SEARCHING FOR AMYLU DANZER

SEARCHING FOR AMYLU DANZER

*

JOHN ROSENTHAL

WAYWISER

First published in 2021 by

THE WAYWISER PRESS

Christmas Cottage, Church Enstone, Oxfordshire, OX7 4NN, UK
P. O. Box 6205, Baltimore, MD 21206, USA

EDITOR-IN-CHIEF
Philip Hoy

SENIOR AMERICAN EDITOR
Joseph Harrison

ASSOCIATE EDITORS
Eric McHenry | Dora Malech | V. Penelope Pelizzon | Clive Watkins
Greg Williamson | Matthew Yorke

9 7 5 3 1 2 4 6 8

A CIP catalogue record for this book is available from the British Library

ISBN 978-1-911379-02-7

Printed and bound by
T. J. Books Limited, Padstow, Cornwall, PL28 8RW

to Helen Danzer

"So we beat on, boats against the current,
borne back ceaselessly into the past."

— F. Scott Fitzgerald

INTRODUCTION BY PAM DURBAN

I've known John Rosenthal since 1965, the year he arrived to teach at the University of North Carolina-Greensboro, and I came to enroll as a freshman, my bags dutifully packed with every recommended article of clothing and accessory on the school's checklist.

Over the next couple of years we became members of the same tribe (he was only a few years older than most of us) that gathered in bars and apartments to talk and talk and talk, "… about Keats and Camus and Faulkner and what was wrong with America, which, among other things, included *Time* magazine, television advertisements, men with briefcases, Bob Hope, Rod McKuen, and best-sellers." That tribe and those talks accelerated my escape from South Carolina into a world where people took books and art and music and ideas seriously, and here we are, 53 years later, (minus the lulls and gaps that life imposes), friends and fellow-writers, still believing in words and images and art, still talking about the books and stories and writers who thrill and move us: Marilynne Robinson, Alice Munro, William Trevor, and above all, for John, Marcel Proust.

"Why do we write about the past?" he asked me recently.

One answer, I think, is that we search the past for images and memories that might cohere into a story that "…reveals the meaning of what otherwise would remain an unbearable sequence of sheer happening," as Hannah Arendt wrote. Meaning, not in the sense of something ironclad or absolute, something more like a meaningful sequence that gathers events into a consequential shape. After he invited me to write an introduction to this memoir, I searched my own memory for what has made his friendship so long-lasting and important to me, because from the beginning he was an influential friend, and that search has led me to realize that the story of how I became a writer could begin with his friendship and those gatherings at the University of North Carolina at Greensboro.

This book, as its name implies, traces John Rosenthal's search for the story of his friend Amylu Danzer's death and for his place in her life, and here, as in most worthy memoirs, the story isn't chronological. How could it be? Our memories lie scattered through time; to force those pieces onto a linear timeline would falsify and weaken the power of the connections among those events, and this is not a falsifying book. In fact, one of the great pleasures of this book, which is full of the pleasures of gorgeous prose and humor and clarifying honesty, is the pleasure of traveling with the writer as he traces how the boy who knew Amylu Danzer and the young man who lost her became the man who remembers her now. It's the pleasure of watching something take shape that works like memory itself, tracking back and forth between now and then, picking up images and events and "questions posed and unanswered" by his life and Amylu's and fitting them into the developing mosaic that I'm calling a story. It's the pleasure of watching him question and doubt, and wish he could correct his younger self, as he does in these lines from a scene in which he remembers the last time he saw a troubled Amylu and couldn't find a way to help her:

And I, the leading man, was ad-libbing.
("Pipe down," I want to say to him, after all this time.)

What I also admire here is the honesty with which my friend finesses the difficulty that men sometimes have in seeing the women they write about as more than projections of their own fantasies and fears. What happens in this book feels like an acknowledgment and a dismantling of that process. One of the book's many accomplishments is John Rosenthal's willingness to look with what Toni Morrison calls "unblinkingness," at himself as a young man beset with a "restless shimmering self-regard" and the way in which his willingness to implicate himself frees Amylu Danzer to emerge as a person in her own right, no longer a mirror in which he sees reflected "the special person I hoped I was."

The greatest pleasure of this book, though, may be how it lingers, and why. For me, writing involves a lot of waiting and listening, and I knew that if there was something I wanted to say about the way the book hung around in my head and made me happy whenever I thought about it or read parts of it again, I'd have to be patient. Sometime during that waiting and listening time, I remembered a talk John gave at the opening of a show of some photographs he took in New Orleans' Lower 9th Ward after Hurricane Katrina. "It's up to the artist to make life as complicated as it is," he said, and I wrote it down, because it felt true in an important way.

After I finished *Searching for Amylu Danzer*, I read that quote again, and I realized that it described the source of the book's lingering power and grace. Because to experience life as complicated as it is, the way it happens in this book, is to be invited to remember that life resists being reduced or simplified. It restores the faith I lose so easily, that our certainties and our stories can always be disrupted by new possibilities.

September, 2020

I

Ours was a young friendship based on the assumption that there was an available destiny full of truth and intensity somewhere beyond the boundaries of what we were being taught by our parents, teachers, and ministers. To get there required discipline and a list of things we should never do. We should never try to be cool, never talk about clothes, and never listen to mood music; we should never believe that money was everything, never learn how to play golf, and never become peevish and responsible like our parents. Our goal, quite simply, was to become artists—or at least the sort of people who set their faces against the grain of American life. When we entered our twenties, we still believed everything we believed when we were fifteen because, quite simply, we'd corrupted each other for life.

"Remembering Amylu"
NPR commentary by John Rosenthal on WUNC-FM, 1992

Amylu Danzer, 1957

WHERE ARE YOU?

Broadway was like a river running through the Upper West Side. It swept up everything, spare vacuum cleaner parts, first editions, maybe Amy.

Amylu Danzer was missing.

A flock of pigeons flew above the campus heading to the garbage cans of Broadway. Mounds of snow lay curbside covered in soot and dog piss. Across the river, the snowy clefts of the Palisades.

I tried to extract Amy out of the cold, thin air. I looked for a slant of shoulder, pitch of head, something coltish and familiar. In junior high school Amy had been my first real girlfriend and I was her first boyfriend. We'd lived on Long Island in the small Great Neck village of Lake Success. What had mattered then? *The Prophet*. Clearasil. Our forty-five collections. One night I'd called the Alan Freed Show on WINS and dedicated "A Rose and a Baby Ruth" to Amylu.

Now she was twenty. A junior at the Rhode Island School of Design.

She was one of the five people in the world I'd recognize in a crowd.

My oldest friend.

Was she looking for me?

I can still hear my mother's voice that February morning: "Johnny, I just got off the phone with Amylu's mother. She wanted to know if you've heard from her. It seems that Amylu has disappeared."

15

Disappearing: a magician's trick. It meant nothing.

She also told me this: that last week Amy's parents had received a call from a staff psychologist at RISD who told them that Amy had stopped talking and needed to take a medical leave-of-absence; that three days ago her parents drove to Providence, packed up Amy's belongings, and brought her back to Great Neck; that yesterday Amy suggested that she and her mother drive to Jones Beach to sketch; that after an hour Amy walked up the beach with her sketch pad and never returned.

The state police found no sign of her.

No one has heard from her since.

My mother insisted that if Amylu showed up at Columbia I should call her parents right away. They were sick with worry. Mrs Danzer thought she might be heading my way.

It was February and Upper Broadway was joyless. The winter had been rainy and cold. Four days earlier Malcolm X had been assassinated in Harlem.

I was a first year graduate student in the Columbia English PhD program and I was supposed to be writing my master's thesis on Wordsworth. I didn't like my thesis and I was beginning not to like Wordsworth.

Where are you? I thought. We've understood each other since we were kids. That was our gift to each other. Don't worry. I'll help you. I won't call your parents. I'll read you "Ode to a Nightingale."

I thought of the whimsical drawing Amy had recently sent me, a charcoal sketch of my car in high dunes, a reference to our summer days at Jones Beach. She'd been silent for months, but then, out of the blue, this drawing. I laughed when I saw it.

I scanned the street. Strangers in heavy coats. In the darkness below, the express train rumbled towards Harlem.

Where was she?

It's almost sixty years since I walked down Broadway looking for Amy, and during all those years images remain, contend with each other—Amylu, at seventeen, bursting long-legged sun-splashed

16

from the waves at Jones Beach, rills of water streaming from her hair; Amy, last seen, walking beside me, heavier, stiff, chalk-faced, mysteriously silent, something of the injured animal about her, stoical, looking away. I keep asking myself the same questions—what happened, why?—and, decade after decade, I arrive at a different answer. I never stop asking these questions. I never stop answering them. I remember what I can.

Amy is the only constant and she never stands still.

Whenever I dream of her, which isn't often, she appears as an enigmatic and radiant young woman. In her presence I feel inadequate and a little pointless. She is breezy with me, abstracted, and I am confounded. She never acted that way. Once I nervously asked her (because I was close to waking) if I were dreaming and she replied, "That's up to you." Once I asked her why she disappeared and she said "A ruse was necessary." Sometimes she says nothing. Sometimes she only smiles.

BLOCKPRINT

My name is John Rosenthal and I am a photographer and a commentator on the National Public Radio show, All Things Considered. *Robert Sheeran, Director of RISD Alumni Relations, has been kind enough to forward my letter to you … I am presently writing a book about a student who attended RISD in 1962-1965, Amylu Danzer, who, like you, wrote articles for the student magazine,* Blockprint *… I am perhaps a little too late for this investigation. Even those who knew her at the time may draw a blank twenty-seven years later. But it's possible that someone has preserved some vivid recollection of her. I'm interested in anything you might remember about this young woman. Did she ever articulate a grievance with the world in a specific way? Did she act strangely, or was she simply quiet? Did her peers ever comment on her sadness? Did anyone think she was ill? Did she have a roommate? A friend, lover?*

1992 letter sent to contributors to Blockprint,
the RISD student magazine

TUTTI FRUTTI

(1957-1959)

Amylu was a year or so younger than me and two grades behind. When I first met her at the Lake Success swimming pool in Great Neck in 1955—a pale, blue-eyed, blond girl, five inches taller than me, who always looked like she'd just arrived at her own surprise party—I was thirteen, and, according to Great Neck standards, literary. I'd read bestsellers like *Marjorie Morningstar* and *Not As A Stranger*, and, unlike my peers who were still reading books about famous inventors, I could talk to a sensitive girl like Amy about the mystery of love. I liked poetry too. Sitting next to Amy under the large oak tree beside the Danzer's screen porch, I read *The Prophet* to her and she would close her eyes, listening carefully.

"Fill each other's cup but drink not from one cup," I'd intone into the bright suburban air. "Give one another of your bread but eat not from the same loaf."

Amy and I agreed: two people shouldn't eat from the same loaf.

We agreed about everything and even hated the same words: golf and canasta, to name just two.

A year later, in 1958, my parents moved to an apartment on the West Side of Manhattan and packed me off to Cheshire Academy, an old and undistinguished prep school fifteen miles north of New Haven—known as The Reformatory among the locals. My ju-

19

nior-high romance with Amy—a matter of love notes, secret kisses, and dancing to Little Richard—couldn't survive long distance, and soon Amy found a local boyfriend.

I was crushed. I couldn't believe it. What would they talk about?

Six months later Amy wrote me a letter and asked how I liked Cheshire, and our friendship began.

I wanted to write letters to Amylu as if I were Holden Caulfield and my pals horsed around like the guys at Pencey Prep, but Cheshire wasn't like that. It was a wilderness of boys, some of whom were dangerously stupid. For a while I was lonely. Then I wasn't. Life became intense, sarcastic, savage, and smart. A semi-wicked English master, an owlish man with quick, stony eyes who waved his cigarette gracefully in the air, told me that Kahlil Gibran wrote sentimental garbage. Another master, a handsome old Irish bachelor with a deep tuneful voice, told me to read Faulkner's *Absalom, Absalom!* and write down every word I didn't know, starting with "circumambient." I wrote letters to Amy celebrating my new gravity. I told her about Norman Mailer who said that Negroes were hip and white people weren't. I also told her I was acting in plays and could do impersonations of Kirk Douglas and Marlon Brando.

Amy had responded to my letters with wide-eyed enthusiasm. From her perspective—a quiet, artistic girl stuck in the 9th grade with whooping boys —I might have been a mountaineer describing the shifting beauty of Italy.

Over vacations we'd get together. She'd take the train in from Long Island and we'd see a movie or my parents would get us tickets to a Broadway show. I'd do my impersonations for her. Recite my lines. Tell her about Ferlinghetti. She'd tell me about her art projects.

I told my mother that Amy was a platonic friend, but she just sighed and said "There's no such thing. Poor Amy."

The author, 1957

SPATTERING PAINT

More than fifty years ago, I stood on a railway platform at Penn Station, searching for Amylu. Where was she? Not wanting to look over-eager, I kept arranging myself in different ways—right hand in pocket, both hands in pockets, head cocked to the left, head cocked to the right, a half-smile, an amused smile, no smile, my eyes scanning the platform, my eyes elsewhere, nowhere, withdrawn, as if I'd been lifted by a thought so engaging that I'd forgotten why I was here or even where I was. Then Amy's pale face appeared in the crowd rushing out of the train, the sweet, artless face of my first girlfriend in junior high—the first girl I ever kissed, four years ago, and now my friend. She hadn't spotted me yet and she wore a concerned expression. Then she saw me and smiled broadly. She waved and I waved back—forgetting whatever pose I'd decided on. As she came towards me, half-skipping, I noticed that her blue beret was teetering and the right collar of her tan trench coat lay twisted beneath the strap of her purse. Amy, as usual, all awry. She was fifteen, past the age when girls showed excitement in public—but not her. We hugged until I let her go, and, as we walked out of Penn Station, she told me breathlessly that she'd just a read a book by Herman Hesse called *Siddhartha*. Siddhartha was a seeker of truth. He'd been a Brahmin but had veered off to find his own path through life.

I didn't know what she was talking about. Brahmin? Path?

It was 1960, a a Saturday morning, just before Easter.

Heading east from Penn Station we walked across 34th Street to

Fifth Avenue buffeted by a playful wind that flattened skirts against the legs of laughing women.

We'd planned to spend a couple of hours at the Museum of Modern Art and then fool around in the city until late afternoon when Amy would catch a train back to Great Neck. On the windy street we chatted and laughed a little too easily. We hadn't seen each other since Thanksgiving and hadn't found our rhythm. (Awkward memories of our junior high romance—love vows and Ricky Nelson songs—still floated in the air above us.)

I was about to launch into my new Brando impersonation when I remembered Chucky D., a kid from Lake Success, and I asked Amy to tell me the details of his mother's suicide. Chucky, who was a year or so younger than me, had always been goofy. When I lived in Great Neck, I used to imitate him—bobbing my head up and down, stuttering the words that began with a "p." I hadn't seen him in three years.

"She killed the dogs too?"

"Yeah. They were in the car with her."

"She attached a tube to the gas pipe?"

"Yeah. And closed the garage door."

"They were huge," I said. "German Shepherds. I remember them dragging her down the street."

I put my hand out in front of me as if I were holding a leash and lunged forward, floppy like a mime. Amy laughed her happy familiar laugh and our self-consciousness vanished.

As we turned north on Fifth, a tall woman in a white leather jacket crossed the street carrying a small white poodle.

"Somebody should shoot that thing—"

"Stop!" Amy said, laughing and leaning into my shoulder. Buses roared by and cars honked and a gust of wind lifted a woman's dress over her face. Garters and a juncture of pink underwear; I looked away, my eyes burning. Then I looked up again. The woman stiff-armed her dress down and offered Amy an embarrassed smile as she passed by.

The wind rattled the canopies of stores.

23

I wanted to do my Brando, but Amy tugged on my arm and I followed her eyes across the street to St. Patrick's Cathedral.

"Isn't it amazing?"

When I was around ten, my Godmother, a Catholic, took me to St. Patrick's and asked me if I wanted to light a candle for the dead. I said yes. She dropped a coin in a box and told me that when I lit the candle I should offer a silent prayer. I lit the candle and prayed for Eddy Duchin, a famous piano player who'd died of leukemia the year before.

"Gothic's my favorite architecture," Amy said.

I didn't know what to say. Who had a favorite architecture?

Amy launched into a puzzling account of a cathedral that had burned down in medieval times and everybody in the town had rebuilt it. A nameless sculptor had carved a beautiful angel in an alcove above the choir loft that nobody would ever see.

"Why did he do that?"

That year at Cheshire I'd played Caliban in *The Tempest* and Coney in *Home of the Brave*, for which I'd won the Best Actor Award in the New England High School Drama Festival. I was a born actor and I knew it and so did everyone else. I didn't want to wait around a few hundred years to become famous. I wanted to make a surprise entrance into the world.

We stared at the soaring twin spires with their stone leaves and arches, their pointed vaults and extravagant round windows, and moved on.

When we arrived at the museum I paid for Amy's ticket. "Two please," I said to the cashier, forcefully enough to forestall any objection Amy might make to my generosity. An awkward moment, which I pulled off.

To be honest, I wasn't thrilled at the prospect of hanging out at the Museum of Modern Art.

"Well," I said as we went through a turnstile, "that was pretty shitty, killing Chucky's dogs too."

"She must have been really unhappy," Amy said.

24

"She had really weird teeth."

"I don't think I ever saw her teeth."

"How do you not see someone's teeth?"

"Maybe she didn't open her mouth wide."

"Jesus, Amy, her teeth opened her mouth wide."

Amy looked at me.

"You think her teeth had something to do with her suicide?"

I didn't say it but I thought ugly people were always in for a bad time. So did my mother, whose father had been a dentist in Tennessee.

Then Amy was standing in the middle of the room pointing the way a child points, almost jumping up and down. She was wearing a dark green plaid kilt (gold pin flashing) and dark green sweater. Her coat was over her left arm. Somewhere there was leather purse with a gold buckle on a flap. Her eyes were bright and she was pulling on my sleeve.

"Look, there it is!" she cried.

"What?"

"Over there!"

Embarrassed, I looked across the room and saw the painting or whatever it was.

"That?"

"Yes! that's who Miss Stevens was telling me about, Pollock! He's avant-garde!"

I looked in the direction Amy was pointing.

"What's avant-garde?"

"It's French. It means, you know, different, something like that."

We stood in front of the large Pollock painting. "What's so different about vomit?" I asked.

Amy laughed. She always laughed at my jokes. But she continued to stare at the painting, her eyes wide and widening.

"He drips paint. He drips paint on canvas. That's so —"

I leaned into the painting. Thin black and white ropes of congealed paint. Bits of bright red paint like blood. Like vomit.

An older man wearing a blue blazer and tassel loafers, and a woman wearing gloves and dark red lipstick, stood beside us looking at the Pollock painting. The woman's cheeks were powdery, as if she'd been in storage; her lips tightened and her nose lifted slightly. The man glowered and offered a make-believe laugh. Then he turned to the lady with the lipstick and said, "Whatever happened to beauty?"

I agreed with him, though I didn't want to.

"You think this is art?" I asked.

Amy didn't answer me, as if she were in church.

Across the room a skinny guy with a goatee was explaining Picasso's Blue Period to his frizzy-haired girlfriend who kept nodding her head as if she had palsy.

Blue period, vomit, faces with three eyes. I was ready to leave.

"Speaking of vomit, I said, "the other night in dining hall this kid from the Dominican Republic got sick and puked on the table. Some of it landed on the guy next to me and he got sick and puked back across the table."

Amy was listening to what I was saying, and smiling a little, but she wasn't laughing. She was looking at the Pollock painting as if she were in love. What a sensitive girl.

I told her how everybody was jumping out of their chairs to get away from the vomit and Mr Jackson was telling everybody to stop acting crazy, even though he was checking his own clothes. "It was really funny."

But apparently it wasn't. Amy continued to smile the kind of smile that could ruin my day.

A museum guard in a dark green jacket with a yellow stripe on its cuff slouched beneath an arch, his arms crossed. His pompadour was black and shiny, the lines of a comb embedded in its high arching wave. He looked sullen and bored and I wondered what he made of all this. Probably not much. A different orbit. A toothpick suddenly drifted from one side of his mouth to the other. A neat trick. The thought crossed my mind that he wasn't going to have much of a future with a toothpick in his mouth. Or was this his future? Giving directions to the toilet, telling idiots not to touch the paintings?

The guard glanced up and saw me looking at him and I looked away.

My future without a toothpick spread before me like a field in soft sunlight.

Did the guard envy me, people like me, with our futures? In college I would read F. Scott Fitzgerald and Thoreau and John Dryden. I would star in plays. The guard probably thought his life was good if he could drive down Broadway in a white convertible with his arm around a pretty girl. Of course that wasn't bad, especially if the girl got his jokes.

CENTRAL PARK

After an hour of drifting aimlessly from room to room we left the museum, with its white walls and quiet voices, and walked up Fifth Avenue towards Central Park. The early afternoon city was bright with a big blue sky and barreling yellow taxis; a white cloud floated like a sleepy whale above Bergdorf Goodman; buses accelerated up and down the avenue, clanking manhole covers.

Cocking my head, I lit a cigarette and let it dangle from my bottom lip. As we walked among the throngs of shoppers, I tried to find the right expression to go with the cigarette.

Bemusement.

Amy looked at me and said, "You look dumb. Why do you smoke?"

I stuck the filter up my nose and turned to her, blank-faced. She laughed explosively, a fifth-grade laugh other girls her age had given up when they started laughing like their parents.

At 59th a shabby man wearing a sandwich board and a crushed fedora urged all passersby to repent

The water, trembling on the high basin of the fountain in front of the Plaza Hotel, fell in warped, clear sheets, shot with rainbows.

The spring wind lifted Amy's hair gently off her shoulders.

Sitting in the park a few minutes later, eating hot dogs, we could hear the seals barking as they performed tricks for the children gathered round their tank. High-pitched laughter spread out across the park, rising and falling in waves. Off to our right, a man in striped pants was juggling bowling pins. Except for his arms pumping up and down he seemed frozen in place, concentrated, his trick a hair's breadth away from collapse.

Amy broke the silence we'd fallen into.

"Do you ever wonder …?"

She stopped mid-sentence and I waited for her to go on.

"Never mind," she said.

"No, what?" I asked.

It turned out that Amylu was upset because the few friends she had were deserting her to join forces with the girls who had access to the popular boys. She wanted to be, if not popular, then at least not alien in a world that had always been friendly to her. Presently she was worried about her best friend Erica, a girl who wrote poetry and loved *A Tale of Two Cities*. Now all Erica could talk about was cool boys and which lipstick went with her complexion.

I'd been at Cheshire, an all-boys prep school, for two years and had forgotten what it was like to walk by girls gathered in front of their lockers, poking and combing their hair, staring at themselves in compact mirrors, applying lipstick, whispering and then shrieking. Girls were actually very dumb.

On the other side of the park's stone wall, a carriage drawn by a horse sporting a red-feathered plume moved slowly down Fifth Avenue, pissing off a hundred cabbies. Above us, the windows of Fifth Avenue apartments reflected the sky, little glinting rectangles of blue behind which lurked grand pianos and rich girls in black underwear.

A young couple flopped down on the bench across from us and began to kiss.

"You really liked that Pollock painting?" I asked, my voice rising into an unexpectedly high register. "He spatters paint. What's so hard about that?"

They were oblivious to everybody around them—the sleeping gray drunk on their right, his head on a newspaper; the French couple on their left, arguing and waving their hands in the air like jerks; and me, my stomach clenched, who couldn't stop staring at them.

The laughter of children burst over the park. Pigeons, darting at crumbs, flew up in the air, then re-settled.

Amy leaned in my direction and said quietly, "They're in love."

I was in love, too, but I hadn't mentioned it to Amy. Her name was Rhonda Glass, and she was a Cheshire town girl who'd played Miranda in *The Tempest*. For the past two weeks I'd thought of nothing but Rhonda, who had a way of looking at my mouth and then at my eyes and then back to my mouth; it made me lose my breath. Even though we'd kissed backstage and talked a lot on the phone, she remained breezy. She could not have cared less about Faulkner or William Butler Yeats.

I wanted to tell Amy about her—I wanted to tell everybody about her—but I didn't.

Compared to sexy Rhonda with her dropping green eyes and half-open lips, Amy was just a girl.

THE AMERICAN MUSEUM
OF NATURAL HISTORY

An hour later, after a long westward walk through the park, we found ourselves standing in front of the Alaska Brown Bear diorama at the Museum of Natural History. The bear towered massively on his hind legs above his smaller mate who seemed to be quietly going about her ground-level, fish-eating business. He looked dangerous, intent, and alive.

Amy asked me if I'd like to be stuffed.

"What?"

"You know, when you die. Like this," she said with a wave of her hand. "You could be stuffed and put in a diorama where your friends could see you."

I thought about it.

But Amy had other plans for me. When I died, she said, I should return to nature and become part of what she called the eternal flow. This eternal flow had something to do with the eternally boring Siddhartha.

It was time for my Brando impersonation—Brando performing Caliban's "sounds and sweet airs" speech from *The Tempest*.

I touched the buckle on Amy's purse. Then, making sure no one was around, I whispered into the air, gently, deliberately, "Be not afeard. The isle is full of noises, / Sounds and sweet airs that give delight and hurt not." I half-closed my eyes, cocked my head, constricted my throat, and reached for the distinct Brando timbre—a reed instrument with a rasp. And wonder too, for Caliban had been struck by wonder. I went on. "Sometimes a thousand twangling instruments / Will hum about mine ears, and sometime voices / That, if I then had waked after long sleep, / Will make me sleep again ..." I paused. I'd found it. I was locked in. I saw nothing in front of me, no dioramas, no Amy—I was drifting on the blind edge of Caliban's confusion. I stretched the pause to an almost embarrassing length. "And then, in dreaming" I continued, "the clouds methought would open, and show riches / Ready to drop upon me, that when I waked, / I cried to dream again."

Amy sighed and said, "That was beautiful."

My best audience. Always.

We walked around the museum for another hour, back in our old rhythm, nudging and teasing each other, floating about in a mild and tender trance that often gave way to silent gazing. The corridors were dark except where the light of the dioramas spilled out. We fell for the faultless taxidermy and the painted back-drops—the wolf's cold winter birch forest, a crag above a sunlit gorge on which a jaguar warily stood. In turn, the museum offered us the full inventory of a lost Eden discovered on the sly. It was a great privilege really—like that moment in the theater when the curtain rises and you find yourself observing what in everyday life you will never see: not only a stranger's parlor with all of its inti-mate furnishings, but a person caught in a wholly private moment, a young woman sitting on a Victorian sofa, crying quietly into a handkerchief.

At Penn Station we paused awkwardly at the top of the stairs that led down to the Great Neck train. Amy retrieved a mashed train ticket from her purse and put her beret on, angling it a little. Her face had gone blank.

"I've had such a great day," she said quietly, looking at my neck. "I wish I didn't have to go home." Her mouth turned downward in a playful pout.

I was suddenly confused. Something was in the air.

People carrying shopping bags hurried past us down the stairway.

Amy and I are friends, I told myself firmly. We talk about books and movies and ideas and I am in love with Rhonda.

She hugged me tightly and I felt her tremble. I watched her as she walked down the stairs, her pale fingers lightly touching the wooden rail as if she were playing notes. On the last step the ticket slipped from her hand. She bent down to pick it up and turned around to look up at me. Then she waved and touched her beret lightly. She stepped onto the hissing train. These moments appear to my memory as a very short film. A film about saying goodbye. Now, all these decades later, that little hesitant wave, lighter than a dust mote, still floats up from the dark platform below.

That night (*The Perry Como Show* over, my mother clearing ashtrays and turning off lights) I went into my room, opened the window, and looked up and down Ninth Avenue. A shower had come and gone and the avenue was empty and rain-slicked. Across the street, lit only by an eerie yellow streetlight, the dark Gothic towers of the Church of St. Paul the Apostle loomed dimly against the starless sky. I thought, ten thousand women are undressing in front of apartment windows and here I am, looking at the Middle Ages. From my parent's TV I could hear the occasional sound of laughter and applause. I got in bed and, as usual, in the privacy of darkness, I opened my mind to thoughts I couldn't put in words. I wondered if Rhonda was lying in her bed naked (her bra draped over a chair), thinking of me, longing for a kiss, and I wondered if Amy had been bleeding at the Museum of Modern Art. Before we left she'd gone to the ladies' room and stayed a long time. If she was bleeding, was it regular blood or is there a different kind of blood for periods? And what female opening did it come from? And why is it called a period? But I had to be careful about opening my mind too wide because other thoughts could arrive and they could keep me awake. Best not to think about some things—like wondering why Chucky's mom killed herself, and how she could have done that to goofy Chucky who'd come home from school and found his mom and their two big dogs dead in the closed garage. Something like that unravels you. Like that big black-and-white painting at the museum today, "Guernica". We kept staring at it, no longer joking around—the bull with scattered eyes and a knife blade coming out of his back, a screaming horse with a spike in its mouth, human limbs lying around, a woman holding her dead baby, and at the top of everything a bare light bulb. Who was Franco? When was the Spanish Civil War? A long time ago. You can only look at something like that for so long before you lose your sense-of-humor, so after a while we left, and had a good time walking around. It had been a really good day, I thought, and Amy is a good friend, somebody I can talk to about almost anything, and now that I thought about it, just before my thoughts drifted into sleep, she wasn't really sad when we said goodbye at Penn Station and really it had been a great day all around.

I looked out the window of the train and saw a young woman of about twenty standing on a small road that divided an immense green field of unharvested tobacco. She was waiting for the train to pass. For a number of reasons I decided to reach for my camera which was in its case on the luggage rack above my head. Here are some of the reasons: (1) that she was, in her loose, blue dress, with the wind playing in her long tangled blond hair, with the mid-day sun brightening the crown of her head, very beautiful; (2) that she reminded me of a passage from Proust in which the narrator falls in love with a young woman seen from a train; (3) that she reminded me of Amylu Danzer, my first girlfriend, who in memory stands at the edge of the ocean in a blue bathing suit, her long blond hair tossing about; (4) and because the road behind her would vertically dissect the photograph in half, while the railroad easement, the fields, and the clean line of the sky would divide the horizontal plane into three equal strips.

But the train jerked forward, and that was that.

from *"Woman Seen From A Train"*
NPR commentary by John Rosenthal
on All Things Considered, 1994

35

FEBRUARY 25, 1965:

NEW YORK CITY DISAPPEARANCE

At best I can piece the day together. Moments are scattered and many are missing. Certain images, though, remain intact—a *Daily News* headline, white clouds stacking above Columbia University's Low Plaza, an unhappy young man reading in a dim room with bare walls. This young man is surrounded by outdated objects, like someone in an old photograph: a portable Royal typewriter, a small bottle of Liquid Paper, a beat-up paperback of Norman Mailer's *Advertisements for Myself.* Above his small desk is a 3 x 5 index card taped to the wall containing the last three lines of Kenneth Rexroth's elegy for Dylan Thomas: "You killed him! You killed him./ In your God damned Brooks Brothers suit,/ You son of a bitch."

There's also a stack of letters on top of a little bookshelf, and, in a cardboard frame, a soft-focus headshot of a smiling young woman with wavy, light-brown, hair—Sharon, the young man's girlfriend for the past two years at Wake Forest College.

In Ohio over Christmas vacation, while visiting Sharon and her parents, he'd given her a diamond ring. The wedding was planned for early July.

That day in 1965 belongs to the young man in the dim room, but the memory of it belongs to me.

No day is like a day that brings bad news.

On the morning of the day Amylu disappeared, I was lying

36

on my unmade bed in Arizona Hall—a graduate-student residence on W. 114th Street—reading the unexpurgated version of Frank Harris's erotic autobiography, *My Life and Loves*. The Hall was old and filled with erratic noises—chairs scraping, toilets flushing, feet flying down a stairwell, doors slamming, distant voices, and a radio that always seemed to be playing Petula Clark's "Downtown." On the floor beside my bed, a cigarette butt floated in a half-empty cardboard coffee cup.

Frank Harris was a cheerful, high-spirited Victorian satyr who wrote lively prose and walked through life with a perpetual erection. Sexual goodwill surrounded him, and I was envious. I'd just spent four years at a Baptist college in Winston-Salem where even dancing could get you into trouble. Sex itself was an act of stealth—reserved for drive-in theaters, secluded forests, and cheap motels with shag carpets.

On the day that Amy disappeared I was fully aroused and, I should add, ashamed—not only because I was reading semi-pornographic literature (mild by today's standards), but also because I was skipping Dr Clifford's course on the Early 18th Century Novel, and, in particular, his lecture on Daniel Defoe's *Moll Flanders*. Academically speaking, this was unforgivable. Any lecture by the ebullient James Lowry Clifford, author of *Young Sam Johnson*, was a gift offered only to the select few, and I was one of the them.

But once you begin to forgive yourself, it's hard to stop. After skimming a few pages, I found what I was looking for. The persistent sixteen-year-old Frank had managed to slip the knickers off young Jessie in her Park Avenue apartment and he was pleading with her to expose her breasts when the pay phone in the hallway outside my room began to ring. I paid no attention to it because Jessie, an obliging young woman, had unloosened her chemise and it was settling in soft rings at her feet. Frank was a convincing young man.

The physicist next door answered the phone, and rapped once on my door.

"Rosenthal, it's for you," he said peevishly.

The hallway was painted a sickly green and I could feel my mother's impatience vibrating through the receiver.

"Johnny, I'm glad I caught you. Have you heard from Amylu?" It was barely a question, the words rushed.

Frank and Jessie and their sweet desire faded away.

"No. Why?"

"I've just gotten off the phone with Mrs Danzer and she was very upset."

Before I could ask why, my mother told me that Mrs Danzer and Amy had gone to Jones Beach yesterday to sketch and they'd gotten into an argument and Amy had stalked off angrily. "She never returned," my mother said, "and eventually Mrs Danzer called the police, who looked everywhere for her but couldn't find her. She'd just disappeared." With a trace of annoyance in her voice my mother said, "Mrs Danzer thinks Amy might have hitchhiked into the city to see you."

None of this made sense to me. Jones Beach? Amy was a junior at the Rhode Island School of Design in Providence.

"Well, according to Mrs Danzer, Amylu was asked to leave school. Something about her not talking, not saying a word to anybody, not to a soul. It sounded strange, but I didn't probe. Apparently her parents brought her back to Great Neck on Sunday."

"Mrs Danzer thinks she might be looking for me?"

"That's what she said. She said you were Amylu's only friend."

"Her only friend?"

"Yes, that's what she said." She paused. "Do you think she was exaggerating?"

I was dumbfounded and my mother was veering.

"It doesn't make any sense to me," she continued, "a young person with only one friend. You can always put yourself forward."

I took a deep breath. As a pretty young woman in Tennessee during the mid-1920s, my mother, Frances Stone, had been charmed by the hijinks of Sewanee underclassmen who favored straw hats and posed on running boards; she regarded introversion as a defect.

A question took shape. "Did Mrs Danzer say anything about

Amy wanting to harm herself? If she was unhappy and was asked to leave school—"

My mother cut me off. "No, she didn't say anything like that. Not at all."

In September, a few days before I moved into Arizona Hall, Amy called me at my parents' apartment on 57th Street in Manhattan. She spoke in a monotone and insisted (she was not a person who insisted on anything) that I drive to see her in Forest Hills, where she was visiting her grandmother. An hour later we walked around her grandmother's old neighborhood, a few blocks from Queens Boulevard. Amy looked pasty and swollen, as if she'd been sleeping too much. She hardly said a word and kept her eyes on the ground. I was puzzled and kept talking to fend off pauses. Why had she called me? She seemed to have no interest in anything I said, and, for the first time in our friendship, I cut our visit short. She more or less shrugged when I said, I've got to go, maybe we can get together over Thanksgiving.

Amy was my oldest friend. Our reunions had always been lively and full of laughter.

A week later she left for her junior year at RISD and I hadn't seen or talked to her since. Over vacations we'd usually try to get together— go to a museum or see a film. Or we'd talk on the phone. But now, for these last five months, there had been silence.

"Okay," I said. "I'll keep a look out."

My mother wasn't through. If Amy showed up, I must tell her to call her mother, who was beside herself. And of course Amy couldn't stay in my room. She may need help and I shouldn't try to be a hero.

"One more thing, Johnny. I assume you've heard about the black minister who was killed the other day? The one with the strange name."

"Malcolm X."

"I think that's it. What kind of name is that? Dad said it wasn't too far from you. Do you feel safe? Maybe you should come here for the weekend. If people want to let off steam—"

"No, it's up in Harlem, Mom. Nothing to worry about."

"Isn't Columbia in Harlem?"

"Not quite."

Then my mother told me that Sharon needed to register her silver pattern soon. "And hopefully she won't choose a pattern that's too ornate. July's just around the corner."

"This is February."

"Our Gorham is simple and elegant. Over the years we've received so many lovely compliments. Now remember, Amylu's not your responsibility."

"Yes, I know."

Back in my room I pulled the cord and raised my window shade and glanced up and down the cold February street. A blond woman wearing a waxy, black leather jacket shielded her face against the wind whistling past Butler Library. She wore the zombie look favored by Barnard students: blackened raccoonish eyes. Above her, behind high arched windows, in the windless world of a vast reading room, students sat motionless at long dark tables in tiny pools of amber light.

Questions passed through my mind.

Did Amy "hitch" a ride into the city from Jones Beach? Amy wasn't the hitch-hiking type. She must have been frantic.

Heading towards me?

How could I be Amy's only friend? The thought was flattering and alarming.

A memory arrived, full of depth and a little unwelcome: Amy sitting beside me on Jones Beach, a towel draped over her wet freckled shoulders, listening as I recited a short poem by Yeats. Dramatically, I'd whispered the final lines—"I have spread my dreams under your feet;/ Tread softly because you tread on my dreams"—and I'd watched the goosebumps rise on Amy's arm.

One question almost took my breath away: wouldn't someone have noticed a fully-clothed young woman walking into the ocean?

40

No, not that.

But where is she? In the city? On a subway. On a park bench?

I picked up the electric toothbrush Sharon had given me for my birthday. I didn't want an electric toothbrush. I wanted the new Walter Jackson Bate biography of John Keats. Hadn't I, more or less, asked for it? What is this thing? Why would anybody use it? I turned on the toothbrush and, for a few seconds, thinking about Jesse and young Frank, I pressed the vibrating brush against my groin.

* * *

This young man in the dim room. This unhappy young man in the dim room. The one person who is left, after all these years, to remember Amylu Danzer.

Odd, how he kept her in mind over the years. (Not often, really. She'd occasionally appear in his dreams, and years later, when he'd become a photographer, she'd sneak up on him in the copper twilight of his darkroom, offering herself, not in the shape of a remembered young woman, but as a series of questions, posed and unanswered.)

I've said I've grown beyond this young man, but, strangely, the more I write, and the more I ask him to narrate this day, the closer I feel to him. I suppose he needs a curator—who turns out to be me. I certainly appreciate the distance between us—how could I not? He lived on one side of history, and I live on the other. Our collective memory of the 1960s almost reaches back to that February day, but not quite. He's hard to retrieve—his voice, his passions and insecurities. Looking through his eyes is tricky. In his America, the Vietnam War was just a rumor; there were no Black Panthers, no drugs, no Janis Joplin, no sexual revolution, no dropping out. Women figured deeply in his world, but never on their own terms. Somewhere there were a few computers, but not many. A few visionaries predicted what was coming, but nobody else. And certainly, the unhappy young man in the dim room was no visionary. Far from it. He was writing a master's thesis on William Wordsworth, and it was going badly.

41

The pall of naiveté hangs over the day.

So what do we need to know about this young man? Can we reduce him to a few details? Not too few, perhaps, but not too many either. He clearly mattered to Amylu; he was, among other things, her first friend. We can't treat him too lightly. He remembers how cold it was the day she disappeared, the threat of snow. That's an odd thing to remember, but he remembers it, and he considers it an important memory. Nobody else does.

The search for Amylu Danzer begins with him on that February day in 1965.

* * *

Unlike most of my fellow graduate students who arrived at Columbia in the fall of 1964, young men and women eager to publish and make a name for themselves (a few had already published articles in obscure literary journals), I wasn't convinced that my adult life was about to begin. I was twenty-one and wanted to loiter. In the early Sixties there were lots of young people who felt that way—people who were about to be stoned for the next five years—but unlike me, they hadn't recently enrolled in the PhD. Literature program at Columbia.

I was told immediately that I needed to specialize my interests, and, a day or two later, I remembered Dr Edwin Wilson, my favorite English professor at Wake Forest, reading to our class from the opening pages of *The Prelude*. He'd read the words quietly and slowly, as if Wordsworth wasn't a venerable poet but simply a man who'd happily escaped from the constrictions of city life, where he'd been "a discontented sojourner." Now he was suddenly free—free to wander about the countryside, his heart lifted by the motions of sky and river and breeze. Beautiful.

I chose the Romantic Poetry Seminar, and, a week or two later, decided to write my thesis on the Gothic influence on Wordsworth's *The Borderers*, a play he wrote before he'd found his memorable voice.

One evening in the university cafeteria, while I ate a cold lump of veal parmigiana, my new (and first) friend at Columbia, B.B. Mulligan, a burgeoning Milton scholar, informed me that, according to Yvor Winters, his senior advisor at Stanford, most of the Romantic poets, but especially Wordsworth, were soft-minded, and syntactically loose—in general, a waste of one's time.

"What?" I said wide-eyed.

I'd never considered that Wordsworth needed to be defended. "'Tintern Abbey'?" I looked at my new pal and said, "'The still, sad music of humanity'?"

The expression on Mulligan's round, freckled face passed from irritation to ridicule. He pushed his large horn-rimmed glasses higher on his nose and said, "Lazy writing. The phrase means absolutely nothing."

I was stymied. What *does* the "sad music of humanity" mean?

As I walked back to my room, the din of Broadway a block away, I wondered if Dr Wilson had been wrong about Wordsworth.

Who the hell was Yvor Winters?

I thought, I'm over my head.

It sounds like a humorous moment, but it wasn't.

The same point was driven home a week later when Roland F., a classmate in my Late Victorian Literature seminar, a large, tweedy somewhat oafish-looking guy, invited me to tea at his apartment. Tea? I said yes. Apparently in the Ivy League one drinks tea and talks about literature.

Roland lived on Broadway a block from campus in a taciturn turn-of-the-century building. His rooms were large and dark and stuffed with old wooden furniture and antiques; the bone china teacup I held self-consciously between my thumb and forefinger felt infinitely too fragile. I wondered if Roland shared the apartment with his mother.

Almost immediately, I felt like a rube. When I told Roland that I'd graduated from Wake Forest College in Winston-Salem, North Carolina, he nodded his head politely and said he'd heard of it. He'd graduated from Yale. Of course it didn't really matter what college one attended, as long as the faculty and library were first-rate. He'd been fortunate in that regard. Harold Bloom, the distinguished literary critic, whom he referred to as "Harold," had been one of his mentors and, in fact, was presently urging him to tackle *Finnegans Wake* at Columbia. Roland made no attempt to be jolly or personal or charming or curious; he simply offered me his credentials as the most authoritative literary mind of his generation. Smoking a pipe, which he used as a baton to conduct his own conversation, he offered me panoramic pronouncements on the merit and/or limitations of a few centuries of writers. Oppositions were apparently necessary. Pope was entrapped by the Great Chain of Being, but Coleridge got lost in the vapors of Christian Neo-Platonism. Faulkner, compared to James Joyce, was merely a regional writer. T. S. Eliot's poetry, which showed signs of plagiarism, was hardly the equal to Thomas Hardy's. It went on.

And there I was again—over my head.

I must have wasted Roland's afternoon, weakly defending writers he so easily dismissed. He was looking for a match, not a bull-session. Yes, I'd read the books, but I hadn't read the books about the books.

As I was leaving I asked about a row of books, bound in red-leather.

"PMLA," he said

I must have looked puzzled.

"Journals from the Modern Language Association. I've been subscribing since I was a freshman at Yale."

Roland was right and I was wrong. He wasn't wasting his parents' money at Columbia; he didn't sit on the sidelines, making fun of pompous types like himself; he wore an air of disdain as if it were tailor-made. He was *all in*—pipe and Harris tweed and a devotion to bibliography.

There was no escaping the unhappiness of that winter, since I was its source. The topic of my thesis was fraudulent, and I knew it. Wordsworth's play, *The Borderers*, was packed with Gothic atmospherics—medieval ruins, raging storms, distressed maiden, and icy villainy. But it wasn't Ann Radcliffe's popular and grossly sentimental Gothic novels ("frantic novels" he later called them), that influenced Wordsworth, it was Shakespeare's *Lear* and *Macbeth*—a richer and more demanding subject. I devoted weeks of my life to citing dubious parallels between high-strung Gothic novels and Wordsworth's unreadable play.

Second-rate scholarship isn't a crime, but it's not good for you.

Some mornings I'd lie on my bed—as I used to lie on a lake, floating, and looking calmly at the sky. Only now I lay like a corpse, barely breathing, staring at the moth fragments clouding the bottom of the light globe above my head. Once, sitting on the edge of my bed, I found myself short of breath with a pounding heart, and, certain that I was dying, I rushed to the window, pulled it open, and, above the noisy, everyday street, gulped cold air. On another occasion I found myself praying, even though the notion of asking a God I no longer believed in to ease my distress embarrassed me, and was a special distress of its own.

As my despondency deepened, I said and wrote nothing about it to Sharon (or to anyone else). In 1965 most young men—at least those like me who'd lived a visibly charmed life—seldom, if ever, paid close attention to their interior life, and were pathetically unprepared for its unexpected collapse. I couldn't admit that I was falling apart, because, frankly, such a failure of self was inconceivable; instead I wore the mask of a witty and somewhat satirical young man—an exhausting performance that fooled everyone except Sharon. Talking to her on the phone I tried to maintain our usual amorous banter, but I was only impersonating the man she was in love with, and perhaps that frightened her; perhaps it bored her. Allusiveness wears love out. Her letters grew monotonous and gossipy; and our great enchantment ("Has anyone loved like this?) turned formulaic. Then her playful anticipation of our married life on a college campus turned sour. "I'm not sure I want to discuss Vital Issues with other faculty wives," she wrote. And a day later, responding to a reference I'd made to Herman Melville in a recent letter, she wrote, "I'd rather have a flowered tablecloth and lie on the beach at Lake Erie than read *Moby Dick*."

I missed the point entirely. A day or two later when I spoke to her on the phone, she told me that Faulkner was unreadable.

"I'll buy you a subscription to The Reader's Digest Condensed Books," I said. "That's about your speed."

She cried.

That morning, after my mother called and told me that Amy was missing, my half-written thesis lay on my desk beside Horace Walpole's *The Castle of Otranto* and a stack of Ann Radcliffe novels. I hadn't looked at it in a week. My brain had closed down in the presence of so many mad monks and satanic villains.

Beneath my window, an ancient steam radiator clanked a couple of times and hissed on.

My Life and Loves, all one thousand pages, sat on my pillow like a toad.

Hide it.

Under my laundry.

Air things out.

I cracked the window, made my bed, plumped the pillow, and straightened my books.

I'll read her Keats.

I thought, it's February, she'll freeze in the city.

I pictured her sitting on the wide steps of Low Memorial Library, shivering: a blue-lipped young woman in a camel hair coat.

I'd approach her gently, tentatively, no shouts or smiles; she'd look up and see me. I'd smile. She'd smile. She'd be fine then.

I flew down the stairs into a bright sunless winter day. Cars double-parked up and down 114th Street. I zipped up my leather jacket against a chill wind sweeping west from Morningside Park. A few snowflakes danced around.

Suddenly I felt like myself again. Not even slightly ridiculous.

* * *

Heading south I walked intently. I felt purposeful and even impressive. As I scanned the street for Amy, I felt sorry for those around me who, with their purses and packages and briefcases and groceries, were stuck in a round of humdrum responsibilities. Compared to them, I could have been the leading actor in a film, a French film, about a young man searching for a woman in a cold black-and-white city.

Up and down the avenue pigeons, like plump, nervous dowagers, warbled and fluttered on the cement balustrades of stout old buildings.

At 110th and Broadway I watched an old woman with ragged gray hair, wearing a thin, worn coat and bedroom slippers, shuffling across the street, eyes flashing but blind to traffic, pushing an empty shopping cart and talking to someone who wasn't there.

I pictured Amy standing on the strip of ocean highway between the dunes and the bay, under a sky that was blue and cloudless. She was disheveled, her face mottled with vulnerability. I pictured a car slowing down, a lone driver, a middle-aged man leaning across the passenger seat and rolling down the window. "Where you heading, Miss?" he says.

At 104th two black men in starched white shirts, black bow-ties and identical black suits walked towards me. Focused and immaculate, glancing neither left or right, they walked down the center of the sidewalk and I made way for them.

On the corner of 101st Street a tallish blond woman in a camel hair coat walked swiftly towards Amsterdam, a familiar swing to her purse. She turned into a building, briskly, a city woman with thin ivory ankles in clicking high-heels. An apartment filled with cold winter light; a lover waiting, impatiently.

A medical-leave-of-absence. What did that mean? My mother said Amy had stopped talking. Was that so bad? Maybe her friends were boring. Mental illness? When I was younger my mother

47

mentioned a Tennessee cousin who was "off" and ended up in the Nashville insane asylum. A nice young man, she said, but "he took liberties"—whatever that meant. Everything I knew about mental illness came from novels or movies. Faulkner's Quentin Compson drowning himself in the Charles, undone by his sister's promiscuity. The hallucinating sexually-repressed Miss Jessel in *The Turn of the Screw*. And a little film I'd recently seen, *David and Lisa*, about two young people confined in a private psychiatric hospital. David couldn't bear to be touched and Lisa, who talked only in dippy rhymes, had a split personality. High-strung artsy stuff with lots of clock symbolism. Eventually they fell in love, which solved everybody's problem. He allowed Lisa to hold his hand, and Lisa dropped her alter-personality and gazed into David's eyes, talking in prose. A fairy tale.

What did I know about mental illness? Nothing.

Had Amylu been falling apart during our last visit in Forest Hills? Had I missed that?

The light changed and I crossed the street in a jostling crowd with tense, chapped, grim, winter faces.

Amy disappeared at Jones Beach? Our beach. The landscape of our friendship. From boyhood on, Jones Beach meant Amylu to me and not much else.

Jones Beach.

The long, endless, dangerous, hot, bright beach a symphony of wave thunder and ear-splitting mock-fright. "No rough-housing in the water!" Amy's mother shouts from the shore—

At twelve. Amy is Bob's tall, awkward, younger sister, knocked down by a wave but laughing, close to tears—

Amy, my teenage girlfriend, cradled in the swells, promise made, I won't let you go, promise broken, tossing her into a wave—Amy kicking, splashing, laughing—my mother, on shore, unsure of this modern tangling—

My Elvis and Buddy Holly imitations on the boardwalk. I want you, I need you, I love you. That'll be the day—

48

Later Amy, my oldest friend, lying on our towels in the sand year after year, the always startling face-to-face sunlit proximity, the down of cheek and minuscule creases of lip, talking of books or movies or my current girlfriend, as we shaped sand beneath our cheeks,

Amy at nineteen, harmonizing "Banks of the Ohio" with me as we pulled into the parking lot of Beach #6 in my Volkswagen.

Amy, quieter over the years.

Jones Beach.

Mrs Danzer had told my mother that I was Amy's only friend. I rarely thought about Amy, and I assumed she rarely thought about me.

I walked and looked and walked and looked; I breathed in deeply, filling my lungs with air as cold as iron. A bus, its interior alight, hissed to a stop on 97th Street, a row of sallow faces peering over the tops of scarves. Across the street a cliff of blank windows glittered above the cold avenue. New York, I thought, is an array of strangers stacked on top of each other, secret lives, most of them unhappy, behind walls—strangers, some just trying to stay warm, riding subways that burrowed through Indian bones. Yesterday a man in the Bronx killed himself with his own bayonet. The city seeped into me. I wasn't a hero; I was a graduate student who thought writing good sentences was adventurous. And who was Amy? A thin-skinned art student crushed by a critique?

I stopped and looked through the frosted glass of Zajac's Fish Market at a row of silvery-red fish stacked on a bed of ice. A thick, red hand clutched a fish and tossed it on a scale suspended above the white counter. The scale swung lightly, tilting to the left. The fish head protruded, its mouth open, aghast.

You can't just walk into the Atlantic Ocean in February. The water is too cold, the waves too high. It was freezing yesterday. You'd pull back, think it over. Virginia Woolf weighted herself down with stones. At Jones Beach there was only sand. Would that work?

Turning west on 95th, a somber, slanting street with a little slice of sky, I walked down to the Thalia, my favorite revival house.

Above the dull wintry street the Thalia's curved marquee glowed like a large jewel. On a rainy afternoon, I'd bought a ticket to see Giulietta Masina in a Fellini double-bill—*La Strada* and *Nights of Cabiria*. Twenty or so people in the theater, pale and serious movie buffs and a couple of old men sleeping. Slouching in my lumpy seat I felt myself, once again, falling in love with Masina, a sweetly damaged, transparent angel, doomed to love the louses of the world. Every few minutes the theater's heater banged into life, sending a shudder through the floor.

It felt colder on the street and I headed back to Columbia.

Wordsworth was still waiting.

Sharon was still slipping away.

There would be no heroics today, no comfort gallantly be-stowed, no phone call to Long Island assuring everyone she'd been found and would be home in a day or two.

Caught by the light halfway across 97th Street, I paused on the traffic island. In warmer weather old women wrapped in kerchiefs gathered on the island's two benches—talking, gesticulating, alert as sparrows. Now, behind a loop of chain, the husks of summer flowers lay in patches of dirty snow.

A fish-white hand appeared out of an uptown taxi window and flicked a sparking cigarette through the air. A small plastic shop-ping bag staggered like a drunk up the avenue, slapping against cars, a wraith among the brake lights.

* * *

In a journal entry dated February 26, 1965, I chronicled the events of the previous day: the conversation with my mother, Amy's disap-pearance from Jones Beach, my fruitless trek up and down Broad-way, and an anxious phone conversation with Mrs Danzer in which she confirmed what she'd told my mother—that Amy might be heading my way because I was her only friend. The entry includes something of a eulogy to Amy—in my words, a creative spirit who refused to conform to society's norms—and a curiously sour and

50

precise memory of an August afternoon Amy and I had spent on a beach at Fire Island. It was our last trip to the beach. In a few days, Amy would be leaving Great Neck for her freshman year at RISD. Why this particular memory is part of that day's journal entry is a puzzle to me. Penance? But there it is.

That morning, I wrote, I was in a bad mood because I'd wanted to go to Jones Beach while Amy insisted we try something new—drive another twenty miles to Bay Shore and catch the ferry to Fire Island. Someone she knew had told her about an unspoiled beach on the other side of a dune. I didn't care about unspoiled beaches. I liked beaches with concession stands.

The ferry ride, I recalled, was choppy, and the dune we hiked across proved unexpectedly wide. Complaints, which I'd recorded in my journal, poured out of me—the beach at Fire Island was empty, the weather chilly, the sky overcast; the waves full of lank seaweed, the picnic lunch Amy had packed included boiled eggs, which I hated, and there was too much time to kill before the next ferry left for Bay Shore.

I described Amy sitting on a large beach towel, holding in her hands the book I was currently reading, a paperback copy of Faulkner's *The Hamlet*. I wrote, "Amy was looking at me wide-eyed, almost reverently, as I stood above her, drying off. Then she said, 'I just read a page of your book and Faulkner described the sun as a silent copper roar.'"

I didn't chronicle the scattering of freckles beneath Amy's pale blue eyes, and I didn't describe her long blond hair, which was still wet and uncombed and draping randomly on her shoulders. I failed to mention that her words lifted my spirit and that I began to tell her about Ike Snopes in *The Hamlet*, an idiot, who confused color and sound, and who had fallen desperately in love with a cow. But I remember it now.

However, I did record this: "A few minutes later Amy wandered down the beach and when she returned she was carrying a piece of driftwood in her hands. She knelt down beside me and offered it to me, wordlessly; I looked at it briefly, nodded my head, and returned to my book. 'Johnny, look,' she said, balancing the drift-wood on her left forearm as if it were an infant, while her trembling right forefinger touched a large whorl. 'It's so beautiful. It's a work of art.' She was whispering as if we were in church."

I remember looking up and feeling annoyed. The mist in the air was turning into a drizzle. We'd be soaked by the time we reached the dock. I'd have to change into wet clothes in the men's room at the ferry. I'd have to drive back to the city with sand in my clothes. What did a piece of wood have to do with the layered beauty of Faulkner?

I'd said, "It's not a work of art, Amy. It's a piece of wood. It has nothing to do with art. It's debris."

I recorded that Amy had said nothing; she just kept gazing at the piece of driftwood as if it contained a mystery that was important to her. Then after a while she sighed and looked at me, and I saw tears in her eyes. I assumed they were the tears one sheds in the presence of great beauty, and for a second I disliked her and her tears. It was all nonsense. It was a piece of wood, that's all.

Amy was reported missing over half a century ago, enough time for me to turn into the kind of person who walks on beaches looking for driftwood. I remember those tears in Amy's eyes reflecting the early afternoon's pale light—as weightless as the apology I would like to offer now. I would say, "I've been a pho-tographer for more than three decades and I appreciate the hard yet luminous beauty that sometimes shimmers on the surface of things. And yet, to be honest, I've never been able to capture the cold, silvered depth of driftwood. Perhaps the story of driftwood is too large for a photograph. Perhaps it is too long. Just think of it—the dying and transforming, the generations of drift. Think of the wood beneath the bark—sun-scorched, then iced, polished by sand, bleached by salt, deformed by waves. To end up where? There, on the beach. On that August day? In your lightly freckled hands? I must have feared the ruthless beauty of your driftwood.

It spoke of depths I wasn't ready for. Were you disappointed in me? Was that moment on the beach a turning point? I'm sorry if I got things wrong. I was a young man. I didn't understand why you had tears in your eyes. I didn't understand your tears were for me. I didn't understand very much then, and it's not at all satisfying that I do now."

SMOKE RINGS

On a sweltering August night Amy and I stood in Times Square on the corner of 44th Street and Broadway. Across the street, the twenty foot face of Sgt. Bilko blew five-foot Camel cigarette smoke rings across Broadway. The air was humid and smelled faintly of horse manure. Theaters were emptying out and well-dressed men whistled for cabs as their wives opened evening bags and searched for compacts. Nobody was unhappy but me, and I was unhappy because we'd just seen *The Music Man* (my parents had surprised me with the tickets) and in 1958, when I was approaching sixteen, I disapproved of musicals. They were trivial and they expected you to drop all you knew about Shakespeare and sit there laughing. I was also unhappy because Amy wasn't paying attention to what I was saying. When I'd declared that *The Music Man* was superficial, middle-class entertainment, definitely not serious theater, she'd merely looked over my shoulder as if she were an out-of-towner hypnotized by flashing neon. "Why should anybody with half a brain care about Marian the librarian?" I'd asked angrily, loudly, hoping to be overheard by a tourist from Iowa. But Amy, apparently unmoved by my question, simply said, "But, Johnny, aren't we middle-class?" I looked up at the smoke ring dissolving over Broadway, took a drag off my cigarette, and blew one against her ear.

Photographs testify to the relentless effacements of time. No matter what the conceptual intent of the photographer—whether it be "serious" image-making or family snapshots—the camera renders with indisputable sufficiency the details and lineaments of its subject: a smooth, fresh, laughing face, the sleek angularity of a new building, a dotted veil worn by a woman coming out of church. Years later—when the young face is wrinkled and the modern building looks corny and nobody wears veils anymore— these photographs tell a story. And who could have guessed what that story would be? The melancholy of Time inheres in photographs, in the resemblance that no longer resembles.

John Rosenthal

Ideas, *publication of The National Humanities Center, 1996*

A CUP OF OVALTINE

The day after I'd learned that Amylu was missing, Friday, February 26, I drove to Jones Beach to look around. I thought there was a possibility she might be hiding in the dunes. It was a quixotic notion—the state police had searched for her everywhere, and two freezing nights had passed—but it was better than sitting in my room feeling puzzled and useless while slogging through *The Mysteries of Udolpho*.

Before I left the city I phoned Mrs Danzer. Had there been any news of Amy? No, she said, not a word. When I told her that I was driving to Jones Beach to look around, she said that was very kind of me, without saying what she probably thought—that I was wasting my time. But who knows what she was thinking, what hope she held out? Then she asked if I'd mind stopping off in Great Neck for a few minutes. It was on the way. I said, sure, of course I would—but I wasn't happy about it. I could imagine only an awkward conversation with the mother of my missing friend.

She opened the door before I knocked.

"Thanks for coming, Johnny," she said flatly, stepping back into the house. I walked past her into the living room, feeling self-conscious in the new role I'd been assigned—that of Amy's special friend.

Mrs Danzer's face looked strained and raw. She wore no make-up, but perhaps she never did. When I was a teenager, her lack of affect led me to think she didn't like me. But that was all right. Unless Mr Danzer was around complaining about loud music, I enjoyed being

56

at the Danzers' house. My mother was charming to my friends, dazzling really, but she didn't want them wandering into the living room where they could break things, and they had to watch their language around her. She thought dirty words were for dirty people. At the Danzers', nobody was particularly prudish about that sort of thing, and I don't remember any room being off-limits—except Mr Danzer's office, where, as I thought at the time, he designed advertisements for Domino Sugar. Their furniture was old and well-used, and if the Danzers owned any treasures they weren't on display.

On that February day, the house was dim and I received the impression that we were alone. I'd never been alone with Mrs Danzer; I'd never had to look at her.

We sat side-by-side on the long living-room sofa while the basement furnace breathed beneath us.

I realize now that as we talked we were both trying to maintain the illusion, which seemed, at least to me, to be crumbling before our eyes, that everything would turn out all right. Amy had been missing for three days. If she hadn't hitch-hiked into the city, where was she? Well, everything would snap back into shape when a chastened Amy called or showed up. We spoke of her in the present tense, which wasn't always easy.

I didn't say much. I sat and listened to Mrs Danzer, looking concerned, but not too concerned, focusing my eyes loosely on the general area of her nose and the gap between her two front teeth. Now and then I'd glance up at her thick glasses, avoiding eye contact.

I realize now that Mrs Danzer wanted to tell me a story. Perhaps I was the only person she could tell it to. A story that might keep bad news at bay.

Beyond the bow-window a rock garden rose gradually above a low stone wall. It looked like a photograph in a beautiful frame.

This is the story Mrs Danzer told me:

On the Friday before Amy had disappeared, the Danzers had received a phone call from RISD. Something was wrong with Amy.

57

She wasn't taking care of herself. She wasn't talking. What this meant wasn't precisely spelled out, but it was something more than the university could handle. A medical-leave-of-absence was necessary.

Everyone agreed that Amy shouldn't be informed of her parents' pending arrival.

On Sunday, when her parents arrived in Providence and told Amy that she'd been asked to leave college, she was stunned and insisted that her parents were mistaken. Call my psychologist, she said, he'd straighten things out, he was her friend. They told her it was the psychologist who'd called them.

Mrs Danzer told me that, after returning to Great Neck, Amy was quiet and kept mostly to her room. Then on Tuesday night, she and her father got into a terrible argument. He told her that he'd made an appointment for her to see a psychiatrist. Amy became angry and rushed out of the room, shouting, "I'm not crazy, *the world is!*" Then she ran upstairs to her bedroom and slammed the door.

Mrs Danzer seemed to reflect on the moment. "Such carrying on," she said gently.

About ten minutes later, Mrs Danzer knocked on Amy's door and Amy told her to come in. She was lying on her bed, propped up on her pillow. Tears were streaming down her cheeks. "She was wearing a white cotton nightdress," Mrs Danzer said, "and she looked like an unhappy little child. I sat down on the edge of her bed and took her hand and asked her what was wrong. When she was younger, I always knew what was wrong with her—mothers do."

Mrs Danzer paused for a moment and I looked up and held her gaze, which was magnified by her thick glasses. My self-consciousness had completely disappeared.

"Amy closed her eyes and shook her head and said, 'I don't know.'"

Mrs Danzer went on: "I remembered when Amy was a little girl and she'd get upset over something. A toy would break, or she and Bob would get into it. I'd always make her a cup of Ovaltine and that would calm her down. So I asked her if she'd like a cup of Ovaltine, it would make her feel better and she said yes, she'd like that."

Mrs Danzer smiled, remembering the moment. "So I made her a cup, but when I returned to her room, she'd fallen asleep. I left it beside her bed and turned off the light."

Mrs Danzer took off her eyeglasses and rubbed her eyes.

The image of Amy as a frightened child in a cotton nightdress was terribly poignant, but I didn't change my expression. Anything else would have challenged our tacit agreement that Amy's disappearance was a problem, not a tragedy.

"The next morning," Mrs Danzer continued, "she came downstairs looking like her old self, very cheerful, and she asked me if we could drive to Jones Beach and sketch. When she was in high school we did that a lot. It was too cold for sketching, but I said yes anyway because I wanted her to be happy. So we drove to the beach, muffled up, and sketched for about an hour. Then we started arguing. I didn't mean to upset her, but I guess she's very thin-skinned these days. I said something about wanting her to get help and she flew off the handle and walked up the beach, shouting she wasn't crazy, the world was. Just what she'd said to her father. When she didn't come back in an hour, I got very worried. And I'm still very worried. I just can't make any sense out of this. Can you?"

The question was too large for me and I felt dwarfed by it. Nothing made sense to me.

"No," I said.

Mrs Danzer looked at me sadly. "Do you know what's wrong with her, Johnny? Has Amylu spoken to you about her troubles?"

For a few moments I was lost. Troubles? Her troubles at RISD? Or something else, something long-standing, perhaps something physical? Something a friend would have been told? I was, apparently, far removed from being that sort of friend, for Amy hadn't mentioned her "troubles" when I saw her in September.

Had she been waiting for me to ask what was wrong?

Because something must have been wrong.

I said, "I haven't spoken to her since I saw her in September. She

59

was pretty quiet then and I was a little worried about her."

I didn't say that on that bright autumn day Amy's face had looked almost extinguished, and that she'd stared at the ground and barely said a word, and that I'd felt insulted.

RECOLLECTIONS

In 1992, the acting director of Alumnae Relations for RISD, Robert Sheeran, gave me permission to post a note in the alumnae newsletter asking for any personal memory or reminiscences of Amylu Danzer, class of '62.

I received two notes from students who remembered Amylu, and one phone call.

The phone call was from a Beatrice M., a dorm mate, who hadn't known Amy very well—at least that's what my scant notes suggest. But she remembered precisely what she had observed at the time. Her brief portrait of Amy—wearing her coat in all weathers, walking around in a daze, no interest in her appearance, sitting and staring at her painting for hours—reminded me of the Amy I last saw at her grandmother's house in Forest Hills—pasty, unkempt, and incommunicable.

Lucy W, a classmate:

I consider myself a "survivor" of those years at RISD. We were overwhelmed by everything and college became a traumatic experience. It was difficult at that age to look as deeply within the self, as was being required of us to do for our 'Art'

For months before she left RISD, Amylu had been going through a profound questioning of her inner awareness. She was a very, very good artist. I admired her willingness to put her energy so "out there." When we go deep within ourselves, it is

61

often difficult to speak out. Amylu became very sensitive before her leaving. I understood it then, and even better now ... She was looking too deeply within herself for answers—answers we all hoped would bubble up through our "Art."

Karen K, a classmate:

I only have one memory of meeting Amylu in person. In our sophomore year ('62–'63), my room-mate, Charlotte, and I decided to start a Bible study group for girls in the large RISD dorm. We put up a notice somewhere.

The only person to show up was Amylu. She seemed to have little religious background and was searching for answers like "Is there a God?" and "What is life really about?"

Her questions were so penetrating, Charlotte and I were hard pressed to come up with any convincing answers. At 22, I didn't know much more than Amylu about such thing. I think today I would have something to say to her.

After the meeting ended, Amylu went away obviously disappointed and downcast. However, I didn't pick up then that she was emotionally troubled. She appeared on the serious side but otherwise OK. I did feel a great disappointment in myself for failing to help someone who had clearly been seeking help. That was the end of the Bible study group. I didn't run into Amylu again as she was a year behind me.

I also received a note from Mike Fink, an English professor at RISD. (I recalled Amy, on a drive to Jones Beach following her freshman year, telling me about her favorite professor who loved literature as much as I did.)

When Amylu was a student at RISD the definition of what it means to be an artist was under siege. To put it a little too simply, a new fixation on celebrity, a la Warhol, and a tendency towards bigness and even sensationalism was challenging an older concept of Inwardness. And Amy, really, was all inward. If she was to become an artist, she'd go deep, not wide, private, not public. Other students, talented and social, were being rewarded for catching on, but Amy was all private pain and hidden genius.

She was a person of keen and poetic intelligence, calm and elegant appearance and beauty, and great promise ... I was shocked by her death and I thought of her afterwards as a sort of symbolic figure—not unlike the merciful girl in Hans Christian Anderson's tale, "The Little Mermaid," who vanishes into the foam and becomes one of the "daughters of the air," bringing health and restoration to those stricken by pestilence. I know it is wrong, stupid, to glamorize dreadful things, but it is my way of rescuing the past and recasting. I do that with lots of things—I can see her face in my mind's eye, her delicacy and dignity, even her handwriting, but the particulars have receded behind the mist of time.

A WORLD OF MY OWN MAKING

Before Amy's body floated up in the Rockaways, I'd gotten used to the idea that she'd committed suicide. But still, I wasn't prepared on that mid-April morning to read a small paragraph in the *Times* that identified "Amy Lou Danzer," 21, an art student, as the young woman whose body had washed ashore in Edgemere, Queens. Moreover, I was surprised to read in the same paragraph that a Jones Beach patrolman had seen her enter the water on February 24 where "her head hit the rocks." Of course this patrolman was a pure fabrication. If Mrs Danzer had been told that Amylu had been seen entering the ocean, not to mention that her head had hit the rocks, she wouldn't have assumed that Amylu had hitchhiked into the city to see me, her oldest friend. (Over time I came up with my own fabrication, that of a kindhearted *Times* page editor—perhaps the father of a distressed child—who had created this imaginary witness in order to suggest, not the grim horror of a young suicide, but the terrible misfortune of a February swimming accident.)

Two days later I received a note from the Danzers confirming Amy's death and thanking me for the many "happy hours" I had given her.

A few hours after I read the notice in the *Times,* Peter K. and I walked to Broadway and drank a couple of beers at the West End. When he left, I drank a few more. Looking around the bar at a dozen or so students arguing and laughing and generally having a good time, I decided that Amylu's suicide had wounded me and I would never recover; I would never be carefree again. (I wasn't bothered by the thought that I hadn't been carefree since I arrived at Columbia.) Then back in my room I wrote a letter to Amylu in which I was determined to craft memorable sentences. These sentences included phrases like "the immensity of trackless Time" and "the bright emanation of friendship." I also spoke of the many ways she had influenced me, made me a better person, even when she was a young girl, and I went on to tell her how much I despised Columbia, and that Sharon, my fiancée, was breaking up with me because she could find happiness only with idiots who read best-sellers.

On and on into the night I wrote my deathless prose.

I also began to tell myself stories—or rather, I tried to imagine my way into the mystery of Amy's death. For it was a mystery. After being asked to leave RISD, and before her parents had scheduled an appointment with a therapist, she'd vanished. Nobody knew what she'd been thinking or experiencing. Her father, in his brief note to me, called her suicide God's "dark secret." So it's not surprising—at least it's not surprising to me—that, lacking all evidence to the contrary, I projected my own unhappiness onto Amy. Almost instantly, I transformed my friend into a wounded and unrecognized artist whose suicide was a rejection of everything contemptible about America.

However, there was another story that I'd tacked onto the first. In this second story, Amy's parents, having miserably failed to understand their daughter and protect her fragile talent, would flee Great Neck in shame. To me, this story possessed an undeniable logic: how could the Danzers continue to live in the home where Amy was born and raised? It would all be too painful and raw and they'd have to leave. I packed their pots and pans, and sent them on their way.

Where had I sent them? A dim house on a dim street. Forest Hills. Yonkers. I didn't care. They had to leave.

BodyWashed Ashore Identified

The body of a young woman washed ashore at Beach 40th Street and the ocean in Edgemere, Queens, on Monday was identified yesterday at the Queensboro General Morgue, Jamaica, as Amy Lou Danzer, 21 years old, an art student of 19 Fox Hunt Lane, Great Neck, L.I. According to the police, she was last seen Feb. 24 at Jones Beach by a patrolman. She had entered the water there and her head hit the rocks.

New York Times, April 14, 1965

66

II

REMEMBRANCE

The various ways Amylu remained behind—mental etchings as enigmatic as hieroglyphs—is the source material of this book. Out of these memories I have constructed a Remembrance, which is a tricky problem for the following reasons:

Because memory distorts the past, often for our own benefit.

Because early memories of happiness are fringed with sorrows that nobody pointed out.

Because most of the people I tenderly remember were wearing masks.

Because something you wrote down forty or fifty years ago has attained the status of a privileged memory, even if you were lying to yourself when you wrote it.

Then there's the problem of data. Amylu died so young. She barely got going before she disappeared. She didn't leave much that was tangible. I have a 1957 post card from her mailed from Bear Mountain when she was thirteen. "All the boys from West Point College come here (o-la-la!)" A few traces of her can be found in photographs. She didn't talk about herself very often. She never kept a journal. Only a few people knew she existed. She never had lovers.

And yet, even if it's true that the passage of time undermines the accuracy of our memory, it also offers us something that was missing when we were younger, and which is necessary for true remembering: the righteous and always late gift of self-mockery. My journals, kept erratically over the years, not only refer to events

I would have otherwise forgotten, but, more importantly, they have provided me, quite inadvertently, with a clear and sometimes comic image of the young man who was Amylu's oldest friend. Without this journal, I wouldn't have had access to the young man who perpetually justified his likes and dislikes, and rationalized his mistakes and inconsistencies. I would have had to conjure him from memory, which often deals in counterfeit goods. But there he is, undeniably, a young man who never could have imagined that when he was in his sixties, his limitations would prove to be the most interesting thing about him—at least to me, the older man, who wants to recover Amylu Danzer, the young woman he spent so much time talking to.

I began with a mystery—that at sixty I knew her better than I knew her at twenty-two, my age when she died.

I began to revisit the Amy I had known, but this time with the questions of an older man.

I polished the lenses of my own self-mythologies, and replaced them.

This book is the memoir of a posthumous friendship.

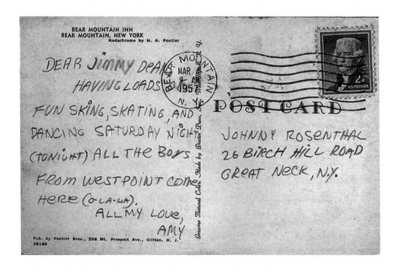

INTERMITTENCY:
THE FORGETFUL YEARS

It's not surprising that as the shock of Amylu's death began to dissipate, so, too, did the mythopoetic notion of her suicide as a defiant act. Artists, I thought, don't kill themselves to make a point; they make angry art and *that* is the point. Wasn't Jackson Pollock, on some level, angry?

Friends said she must have been mentally ill, as if suicide itself is proof of mental illness. I didn't quite buy that, but I didn't argue the point.

Yet soon the main fact about Amy wasn't that she'd committed suicide, it was that she was *gone*, and then more and more gone—a receding figure—someone waving at me disconsolately as life sped up and I rushed into the Sixties.

In August, 1965 I said goodbye to my parents, tossed my clothes and books into the backseat of my Volkswagen, and drove down Rt. 1 to North Carolina where I would soon begin my job as an instructor of English at UNC-Greensboro. I left behind a year of losses—Sharon gone, Amylu dead, my sense of self-worth diminished. However, I was twenty-two years-old, single, modestly armed with a master's degree, and in a week or two I would receive an extravagant paycheck of $550. I knew three auspicious things about UNC-G:

(1) that until 1963, which was the first year males were admitted to the general student body, UNC-G was known as Woman's College.

(2) that its present student ratio was about ten females per one male.

(3) that two writers whose work I admired, Randall Jarrell and Peter Taylor, would be my colleagues.

A few days before classes started, I found a cheap apartment off Church Street, bought a sleek, white Honda CB160 motorcycle, a Motorola stereo with detachable speakers, and two record albums—the Rolling Stones' *12 × 5* and Bob Dylan's *Bringing It All Back Home*.

My job consisted of teaching five classes of young women how to read literature with a critical eye, and to write intelligible sentences. One autumn day, while I was standing behind a podium in front of a class of sophomores, pointing out some of the reasons why the governess in *Turn of the Screw* might not be a reliable narrator, I looked around the room and saw a congregation of young women, looking at me and listening intently to every word I said. They were all wondering, as I'd once wondered, if the governess, who appeared to be a perfectly decent young woman, was in fact insane; they were wondering if a famous book could really trick you like that. For a second I saw myself standing there in front of them, a courier of enchantment, and I thought: I better keep this to myself—if it gets out that somebody's paying me money to talk about Henry James to these young women who lean towards me as if I'm whispering secrets in their ear, I'll be fired and have to work at the Vicks factory across town. Which might explain why, after two months of teaching, of charming and being charmed by my students, I began to think of my terrible year at Columbia, which ought to have been a chastening experience, as nothing but a brief disturbance on my happy journey through life.

For the next three years I talked to my students, in bars and classrooms, about Keats and Camus and Faulkner and what was wrong with America, which, among other things, included *Time* magazine, television advertisements, men with briefcases, Bob Hope, Rod McKuen, and best-sellers. These conversations resembled my early conversations with Amylu back in junior high, though the objects of my contempt had been updated. I fell in love with a couple of my students, but that was okay—they were largely playful affairs that led to enduring friendships.

What I do regret, however, were those occasions when my love of literature turned into self-lyricism and I spun the story of Amy's death to a flirtatious advantage. One late winter afternoon, while hanging out with an older student in my apartment, drinking beer and smoking grass, I read her Keats's "La Belle Dame Sans Merci." I read it quietly, almost tonelessly, letting the words and only the words depict the desolate drama of the poem. Honestly moved, I told her about "my friend Amylu," a young woman, only twenty, who'd walked into the ocean two years ago and drowned herself. The connection between the poem and Amy was spurious, but it worked. Stoned, my student looked at me tenderly, as if, like Keats's knight, I'd experienced more than my share of sorrow—a man alone in Greensboro, a lily on his brow, palely loitering.

Of course Amylu continued to vanish in the way the dead do. There's just so much they don't know. *Rubber Soul*, for instance. Amy had never heard it.

Then came Lyndon Johnson and escalation of the Vietnam War. Then drugs, the Anti-War Movement, Students for a Democratic Society, Angela Davis, Otis Redding, Abby Hoffman and assassinations.

For a while I became a member of a new and vivid mob.

"What in God's name has happened to your vocabulary?" my friend Clough asked me on the phone. Clough, who was the angriest person I knew, lived in Boston, and we wrote letters to each other at least once a week. Writing well was the point of these letters—to write about books and films and our messy lives with some measure of cynicism and eloquence. Clough continued, "In your last letter you wrote 'Antonioni's *Blow-Up* is "far out" and Mailer's new book is "a bummer"?' Jesus, man, are you turning into one of those idiots?"

I was.

Nixon had arrived, and in 1968 I was offered a Teaching Fellowship at UNC-Chapel Hill.

There was now an old world, and a new one, and Amy belonged to the old one. A lot of people belonged to the old world

TWO SNAPSHOTS

March, 1969

I am sitting on a bed in a rented old farmhouse outside of Chapel Hill, and beside me is Susan B., a pretty young woman from New Orleans, a former student of mine at UNC-G. We're high on mescaline and we're trying to decipher the hidden meaning of Dylan's "Sad-Eyed Lady of the Lowlands." Nothing seems more important than getting to the bottom of it. Was the sad-eyed lady Joan Baez? Or was she Mimi Farina, Joan's sister? We debate the issue. In a couple of months I'll marry her at the local courthouse. My friends will arrive in clownish clothes, tripping; my wife's New Orleans grandmother, a sheltered, angry old woman, will faint and be revived with smelling-salts; and I'll read a William Meredith poem that celebrates the power of lovers "to aid and injure one another."

May 6, 1970

Following the killing of four unarmed Kent State students, six thousand angry and agitated UNC students had gathered on the main quad of the campus.

I was the first speaker.

Leaning into a microphone, I spoke quietly, persuasively, trying to crystallize the reasons why these politically naïve students should oppose a government that dropped napalm on children ten thousand miles away. When I called for a massive student strike "until the university condemned the war in Vietnam," the students roared their approval.

I believed every word I said, but I also believed in the role I had chosen to play, and I watched myself approvingly—as if from a great distance—as I performed it.

While the four of us spoke, a small group of Yippies, inflamed by the political theatrics of Jerry Rubin and Abbie Hoffman, chanted "Ho! Ho! Ho Chi Minh!"

A few days later the Faculty Council passed a resolution, which avoided any condemnation of the Vietnam war, but granted some sort of amnesty to students who hadn't attended classes after May 6th. It was a weak conclusion to the strike, but it wasn't humiliating; and the thousands of students, who had surrounded Hill Hall where the Faculty Council was meeting, grumbled, shouted a few slogans, and returned to their dorms. The National Guard troops, who had mustered at the nearby Horace Williams Airport, returned the one bullet they'd each been given, and demobilized.

It was a remarkable time in all our lives. Like thousands of others, I'd fallen for the illusion that the good guys were about to win. Wasn't it obvious? "Come on people now," we'd sing, "Smile on your brother/ Everybody get together ..." Whatever insight I'd gained through literature into the dark and ambiguous nature of existence, of the precariousness of joy, was briefly replaced by faith in a stoned future that would address the harsh inequalities of capitalism.

It's not surprising that under the sway of such a politically charged counter-culture, I made less room for Amy, the memory of her, the loss of her, the *singleness* of her. Compared to the systemic mistreatment of millions, the personal torment of a young, middle-class, white woman could feel almost trivial. The lone young woman on the beach, her interior crumbling, was relegated for a while to the shadows.

The author, 1970

SO LONG

From that point on, in the hallowed halls of Academe, I was considered *persona non grata*. The university attempted to revoke my Teaching Fellowship, but collided with the not inconsiderable issue of "academic freedom." Pressing on, the English Department assigned a senior faculty member to monitor my classes once a week—presumably to ensure that the Ancient Mariner's moral failure wouldn't be equated with America's.

I thought, this is all wrong for me.

In the fall of 1971, I stepped away from the university and never returned. My wife and I cashed in our savings, bought backpacks, sleeping bags, a tent, and one-way tickets to London. (In a few years, my wife, who was not a quixotic person, would organize her life around the imperatives of her own personality, not mine, but in 1971, when she was twenty-four, she was willing to risk everything so I could visit Hampstead Heath where a dying Keats had written "Ode to a Nightingale," and, weeks later, stand silently with me in Crete beside the grave of the poet and novelist, Nikos Kazantzakis. I didn't consider that was a lot to ask.)

After London and the Keats House, we hitched into the Lake District where Wordsworth and Coleridge had composed *Lyrical Ballads*, and then spent a couple of months hitching around Scotland, France, Italy and Germany, always edging our way toward Athens where we could catch the Piraeus ferry to Crete. Twenty minutes after we'd docked at the port of Heraklion, we stood on the Venetian ramparts beside Kazantzakis' grave. I held in my hand a copy of *Report to Greco*. The fronds of nearby palm trees clicked together in the early morning breeze, and above us starlings, hundreds of thousands of them, swooped and rose and fell in mysterious parabolas. The gravestone was nameless but below a simple wooden cross was the inscription I'd traveled five thousand miles to see: "I hope for nothing. I fear nothing. I am free."

On a long winding street in the steep hills above Rethymnon—fifty miles down the northern coast of Crete—we rented a small cinderblock house containing a few sticks of furniture. The stove barely worked and the toilet backed up; the furnace gave out and cold air leaked through cracks in the wall. A week-long southerly wind wore us down. A shepherd's dog barked all day. When it turned colder, we argued but slept zipped together in our sleeping bags.

Below us, the sullen Mediterranean spread outwards towards the Greek mainland. Early in the morning a low fog stopped abruptly at the shore.

I wrote poems, kept a journal, and, borrowing a camera from a fellow American, photographed sheep and all the children in the neighborhood.

Occasionally we'd hang out with the few Americans who passed through Rethymnon, stopping only for a day or two. Some were drop-outs searching for exoticism (soon they'd take off to Turkey to buy sheepskin coats and hash); others came for the sort of experiences they could write up in a journal, or to see the ancient Minoan ruins, or to visit the caves of Matala that Joni Mitchell sang about in her song "Carey." A few American women came to dance in tavernas with Greek men whose black-garbed wives stayed home to tend children and sweep floors.

Ill-assorted though we were, we'd occasionally gather in cheap restaurants where a few drachmas could buy you a dish of moussaka and a couple of bottles of retsina, and we'd talk lightly and comically, the way travelers talk whose paths have briefly crossed.

With one couple, however, a deeper note was struck. John and Jane Whiston, recent Yale graduates, were politically committed leftists who were smart and argumentative. Until meeting them I hadn't realized how much the daily disorientation of travel had dulled my mind. So I felt blessed to be able to argue again, and to disagree with people, to be irritated and irritating. Once an argument grew so ferocious that Jane left the house in tears. How could Democracy survive Nixon? Should we respect the revolutionary tactics of the Weathermen? Could Henry Miller, a great writer, be simply dismissed—as Kate Millet had done in her recent book *Sexual Politics*—as a misogynist?

I suppose in retrospect we seem naïve—young, privileged Americans arguing about literature and politics in a country ruled by a brutal military junta. But that would belittle the impulse that brought us there. We weren't giddy vacationers living the good life. We were enthusiasts. We wanted to see the island that Kazantzakis had so loved, with its flowering almond trees. We wanted to walk around the Minoan ruins at Knossos, and the palace at Phaistos rising above the Messara Plain. We wanted to talk to Cretans, to know why they shouted "Freedom" when they danced. We took notes, lots of them. The Greeks had invented literature, and we knew it.

(When John and Jane divorced a few years later, Jane took back her family name and became known as the writer Jane Smiley.)

Shortly after we'd arrived in Rethymnon, I dreamed about Amylu. I don't know if it was the first time she'd appeared in one of my dreams since her death, but it was the first time I wrote about it in my journal. In the dream I was wandering around the Dixie Classic Fair in Winston-Salem when Amy's brother, Bob, came out of a tent and greeted me. Full of gossip, he told me that his sister—he called her Boo Boo—was married and living in Sydney, Australia, and that she'd caught a disease and lost a lot of weight. She weighed only a hundred pounds. I was sorry to hear that but I was happy that, having lost contact with Amy for many years, I could now find her. I wondered why we'd lost contact. I woke up a few seconds later, my arm around my sleeping wife, still wondering, and then I remembered that we'd been out of touch because Amy had killed herself. The sharp happiness of the dream disappeared in a wave of sorrow.

RED BIRD SOON IN THE MORNIN'

1972. On a bright April morning in Crete, I was hiking up the steep dirt road that led from the small coastal village of Plakias to the tiny village of Selia. Ahead of me, on a shady patch of road, a red bud tree had spilled its pink-crimson petals on the dark earth. As I stepped around them a memory arrived that didn't belong anywhere near this warm, fragrant day. It wasn't a memory I'd sought. It found me.

I continued walking up the hill, but I was no longer in Crete, no longer surrounded by chestnut trees and wild orchids and roadside poppies; I was standing with Amylu on a cold winter night in 1962 outside the Gaslight Café in Greenwich Village. The café had been hot—sweltering even; and now, outside, the cold air stung our faces. Amylu, I remembered, was wearing a camel hair coat with a long red scarf and a black-and-white woolen beanie that sat crookedly on her head, its tassel like a black carnation.

She was probably seventeen, a senior at Great Neck High.

Across MacDougal Street, the awnings of the Caffe Reggio snapped like sails.

Earlier that evening we'd had dinner at Livorno's, an old Italian restaurant on Thompson Street where local families dined and played bocce ball on a dirt court. There were leather-bound menus and faded murals of shepherds wandering around Roman ruins and waiters bending over tables with pepper grinders. I'd wanted to show Amy what the "real" Greenwich Village looked like—not the tourist mecca of 8th Street—and Livorno's was a good place to start.

Over spaghetti and meatballs she described her final senior art project to me. She was, in her child-like way, excited about it, and even though I was barely listening, I enjoyed watching her light up and stumble over her words. Her project had something to do with *Siddhartha* and learning Gothic calligraphy and making a book out of rice. I waited until she was finished and then I leaned across the table and quietly delivered Hamlet's soliloquy "O what a rogue and peasant slave am I ..." I'd practiced it in my mind while she was talking.

That fall I'd played Hamlet at Wake Forest.

Since she was twelve, Amy had been my best audience.

After dinner we walked a couple of blocks to MacDougal, then down a flight of stairs into the Gaslight where a solemn gray-haired poet, his glasses perched low on his nose, sat on a stool chanting a poem about atomic annihilation. We took our seats at a small table and ordered espresso. The poet read a couple of more poems about death and then, happily, he was finished, and everybody snapped their fingers because applause, which bothered the upstairs tenants, wasn't allowed. A few minutes later, Dave Van Ronk, a big bearded lumberjack of a guy wearing a black leather worker's cap, stepped onstage, and strapped on his guitar. Tuning up, he talked about Mississippi John Hurt, whom he called "God," and then he sang "Spike Driver's Blues" and a couple of Lead Belly tunes. His fingerpicking was delicate but powerful. He was funny, wry, and political, and his rendition of "The Ballad of Joe Hill" made you feel that Joe Hill had been framed and executed a week ago. He mixed in a bunch of murderous English ballads, growling and whispering, and he ended his set with "On Top of Old Smoky, which he sang darkly, like a poetic lamentation.

"The grave will decay you and turn you to dust," he sang quietly to a room in which coffee cups no longer clinked. "Not one boy in a hundred a poor girl can trust."

Then we were outside on the cold street, bundling up.

Little mounds of snow lined the curb, and Seventh Avenue, a block away, brightened the sky above the Minetta Tavern. As we walked briskly towards my car a few blocks away, I gripped Amy's arm, pressing against her for warmth. Slowing down for icy patches between shoveled doorways, we talked with our heads bowed against the wind. Ahead of us on Bleecker, Figaro's was lit up and packed. It was tempting, but I was already flying with caffeine, and, anyway, I had to drive Amy back to Great Neck by eleven.

Turning left on Bleeker, I glanced at Amy. Bright eyes, red cheeks even under the street light. A merry girl who admired everything about me—but luck had always come my way. Up the block voices and laughter as The Bitter End emptied out. I began to sing, imitating Van Ronk's hoarse voice: "Red bud, tune in the mornin'." I let Amy's arm go and slid along the sidewalk on an ice slick. "Redbud, tune in the mornin, redbud!"

It's not "'red bud,' Johnny!" Amy said laughing, "it's 'red bird'!"

I kept on singing and sliding. Was she right? "Well the cat got the redbud tune in the mornin'."

"And it's not 'tune in the morning,'" she protested, "it's '*soon* in the morning'!"

I didn't care … I kept on laughing and singing and sliding.

I still sing it that way, fifty years later. Redbud tune in the mornin'.

It's a beautiful lyric.

So it wasn't surprising that a blooming red bud tree in Crete reminded me of that night in the Village with Amy, but it was surprising that the memory wasn't altogether a happy one.

Of course suicide darkens remembrance, but more—this memory, which I didn't seek, and which sprang full-blown from a scattering of red bud petals, arrived on its own raw terms, unmediated by a later maturity; it arrived with its cold weather and overheated coffee-house, its awnings, winter coats, night sky, slippery streets and a young man who turned out to be me.

For a moment I fully inhabited that young man—and I saw him offering Amylu the gift of himself, secure in the belief that his talents, playfulness, conversation, soliloquies, the books he'd read, his future plans, even his present love life, were enough for her. More than enough. He was luxurious in his gift-giving, always had been.

Had she noticed that he was bored every time she tried to tell him about her life, her art, her enduring interest in Herman Hesse and *Siddhartha*? Or had she expected that and nothing more?

How would he know? He never looked closely at her.

What had she expected?

I don't know.

Even as we walked down MacDougal Street, huddled together against the cold, I'd tried to reclaim her attention, which I was afraid had wondered away from me.

"Don't you think," I asked her, "that Van Ronk, with his boots and beard, his Paul Bunyan shirt and that New York accent, was a little bit of a phony?"

(Years later I bought a Smithsonian Folkways recording of Lead-belly singing "Red Bird." It's one of his children's songs, also a game song. When he introduces the song he says, "They gonna sing, they playing in a ring, they singing and playing "Red Bird Soon in the Morning."" But a Lead Belly children's song isn't like anyone else's. The red bird, he sings, is "soon in the morning," but then he asks, "What's the matter with the red bird, soon in the morning?" The answer to the question is that a cat, and then a hawk, "got" the red bird. "Red bird's gone, that's soon in the morning." The song has picked up momentum and I can imagine children holding hands and laughing and circling around, faster and faster until they are out of breath.)

A few months later my wife became pregnant and told me she wanted to return to America—to be closer to her family and to American medical care. We left Greece and returned to America, to North Carolina. When our baby was born, we named him John Keats Rosenthal.

I said to my wife, "How do we do this?"

She replied, "I know as much as you do."

Our extended childhood had come to an end.

At some point in the drug-haunted 1970s, after so many friends of mine had lost their focus, or wandered off, or died, my memory of Amy's suicide acquired a fictional tone—something out of a Thomas Hardy story I'd read in college. A solitary young woman on a windswept coast, to whom the Fates had been unkind. Amy's suicide hadn't occurred in the glossy and charismatic rock n' roll era of cultural, fan-driven self-destruction. It had taken place quietly, unobserved, misunderstood, in the less dramatic realm of plain Despair.

AMY'S RETURN

As I moved into my thirties and forties, becoming a parent and a photographer, I hardly ever spoke of Amylu. None of my friends had known her, and, really, it was long ago—and doesn't everyone past a certain age have their own sad stories to tell? I didn't want to swap Amy in and out of that kind of conversation. My life and my friends' lives were crowded with children and careers and aging parents, and that's what we talked about. It wouldn't have been graceful to insist upon the particular pathos of this one suicide, or even hint at the old disquietude that surrounded her death. (The disquiet, however, did linger. Other friends had died, but in death they remained quiet; their absence was a melancholy fact which raised no questions; they didn't appear in dreams that began in joy and ended in bewilderment.)

I wrote essays for journals and magazines, delivered commentaries on *All Things Considered.* My subjects were eclectic—the melancholy of old photographs, the aging of parents, the tyranny of the art world, the narrowing of modern consciousness, the ethical problem of photographing strangers, the endless lies of advertising, the voyeurism of the camera, the sterilities of conceptual art, the way photographs stole your soul—but I rarely alluded to my friend's death.

If I found occasion to speak of Amy's suicide, the story I'd tell was like driftwood in a suburban garden—edges rounded by time and bearing the faint aura of a relic.

I think now that the enigma that was Amy was simply waiting

for the right time to present itself and say, "It's time."

One afternoon in the mid-1980s, I was working in my darkroom (my wife and I were divorced, and I'd been a photographer
for over ten years) when my son, an eighth grader who'd just come
home from school, knocked on the darkroom door, startling me,
and asked if he could take guitar lessons. I was working on a difficult photograph, so I shouted through the door, "Everybody plays
the guitar! Don't bother me! Read a book," and I returned to my
photograph.

A few minutes later I thought: friends of mine don't say that
sort of thing to their children. They want to be friends with their
children. They don't grow impatient. They sit down with their
children and have discussions and listen in a civilized manner.
They believe in "parenting." A child's psyche is at stake.

Yet as I worked away in my darkroom, I began to think about
the delicacy of a child's psyche. God knows I didn't want to harm
Johnny's psyche, and yet, I wondered—is a psyche so easily at
stake? Is the psyche so delicate? Does it need such continual attention? Did Abraham Lincoln's psyche need such consideration?
Emily Dickinson's? My son, in his own determined way, and often
without my help, kept merrily growing up, and I wasn't surprised.

I tried to remember the parents of my Great Neck friends. How
carefully did those parents tend the psychic garden of their children? Unfortunately, all I had to rely on was a boy's memory, a boy
who left Great Neck when he was fourteen and saw only what he
needed to see. A boy without a neutral gaze.

Then, not surprisingly, my thoughts turned to Amy and her
parents. Clearly, Amy had ended up psychically damaged—and,
for a while, I'd blamed the Danzers for her suicide. Why? What had
been their parental crime? Had I been reading R. D. Laing at the
time? He'd written that families could drive their children crazy.
Did I believe the Danzers had driven Amy crazy? Did I ever believe
Amy was crazy? Mrs Danzer stayed at home, cooked, gardened,
and painted landscapes. She had her limits when it came to teenage

nonsense, but she never yelled. Wasn't she a loving mother? Mr Danzer was grumpy almost all the time, but so were most fathers, those poor commuters.

I'd never sent a condolence to the Danzers after her death. I must have been angry.

The Danzers didn't understand Amylu. But that's not a crime.

My parents didn't understand me.

I understood my son now, but in a few years I wouldn't. His secret life would begin.

So many years since Amy's death. What had I forgotten?

Around that time the seventeen year-old child of a friend of mine, a brilliant, playful kid who earned pocket money cutting mats for me after school, suddenly, and without warning, slipped into mental illness, and I thought, nobody can protect their child from that.

Then one night in the late 1980s, I dreamed of Mrs Danzer. She and I were standing on the shore of a beach waiting for Amy to make an appearance. As we scanned the ocean for signs of her—blond head bobbing amidst the small jittery crests, pale arms churning the water—a warm wind blew in from the direction of a hazy and slightly puzzling city we could see on the horizon. As we talked, Mrs Danzer began to change shape. One moment she looked like the middle-aged woman I'd visited in 1965 a couple of days after Amy had disappeared, and the next moment she was only a large face, an unmoored planet drifting silently before me, eyes like round lakes, the gap between her front teeth a remarkable rift. She said Amy had been furious with her that day, and had stalked up the beach, sulking. As Mrs Danzer and I talked—and as her face floated in front of me—Amy suddenly showed up, not out of the waves as we'd anticipated, but rather whimsically and cheerfully stepping down from the dunes. It was a good-humored Amy. Naturally I asked her a lot of questions, which she answered offhandedly. No, she hadn't killed herself, she'd just gone away. A ruse had been necessary. She shrugged. But why, I asked, hadn't she

89

let me know she was alive, sent me a sign from wherever she was hiding. Hadn't I been her oldest friend? Amy laughed, like I was a boy holding a water pistol; her breeziness confused me. I asked if she could stay, here, with us, but she didn't bother to answer. Her nonchalance was unshakable, and I wondered if she were being polite—as one is polite to a stranger who claims to know you. But I had an important question to ask: what about the dental records that had been used to identify her remains? Who did those teeth belong to? As I broached this terrible question, the dream slowed down, and then, like an old tapestry in the hands of looters, it fell to pieces.

When I woke from my dream Mrs Danzer's solemn face—enlarged, as if telescopically—still floated in front of me. It was the face of a parent whose child had run into very bad luck.

A week later I spent an hour in the university library looking for a Robert Danzer in the phone books of New York's five boroughs, but I had no luck. Where had they gone?

YOU'RE STILL A ROMANTIC

"She built a sand castle and then walked into the sea. She may have left a note but I don't remember. The sand castle really stood out in my mind."

From a 1992 letter sent by Karen K,

a writer on the staff of *Blockprint*

M y darkroom. April, circa 1990. I was working on a photo-graph of a gull's elongated shadow as it passed over the dim-pled sand of Crane Beach, northeast of Boston. I wondered if the photograph was too wispy. I couldn't tell yet. A part of me said it was just subtle; another part said it was effete.

The phone rang and I picked it up and a friendly long-distance voice asked if I was John Rosenthal.

"That depends."

Laughter, vaguely familiar.

"The same Johnny Rosenthal who lived on Birch Hill Road in the 1950s?"

Johnny?

"Yes."

"Well, Johnny," the voice continued, but not before taking a deep breath, "This is Allen Raiken. We used to be best friends."

For a few years in the mid-1950s, before my parents sent me to prep school and bought an apartment in the city, Allen Raik-en had lived a couple of houses away from me in the small Great

Neck village of Lake Success. I remembered him as a handsome, funny, self-assured kid with blue eyes and thick black hair. His parents treated him with exasperated adoration, which I envied; he could get away with things. Once, I recall, Allen was angry and said "Shit!" in front of his mother. I'd stood a little off to the side, holding my breath, wondering what Allen's punishment would be. But Mrs Raiken merely shook her head and sighed.

"Too permissive," my mother would say of Allen's parents, as if their son, a star in every possible way, was turning out badly.

During those years, I wanted to be his best friend, but there were always a couple of boys ahead of me.

"It's nice hearing your voice again," I said lightly, sweetly, all grievances forgotten. His voice summoned up the witty, confident boy whose style I'd not only admired, but emulated. In those years I'd pace around my bedroom trying unsuccessfully to catch the tone of Allen's melodic and perfectly-pitched irony.

Was he calling to apologize?

Allen told me he was an attorney in D.C., specializing in commercial banking law; he bought and sold banks for his clients. He lived in McLean, Virginia; was married to a lovely wife, had two lovely children, a son in high school and a girl in middle school, and he owned a boat docked at Annapolis. Normally I tune out this kind of inventory, but on that bright spring morning I was content to drift along on the strangely familiar rhythms of Allen's voice. He was a man who bought and sold banks for his clients, and I was a middle-aged man who had no idea that banks were for sale.

Nothing had changed.

Detecting my admiring tone, he asked, "Well, how about you? What are you up to after all these years?"

I didn't tell him that I lived in a rented house, drove a used car, and that my second wife, too many years my junior, had recently moved to the mountains to become a potter. Instead I told him I was a photographer and a writer, which sounded just fine.

"I do all sorts of things. A play of mine was recently produced at the Playmakers Theater in Chapel Hill. I freelance, exhibit and sell photographs, write essays and book reviews for journals—that sort of thing. I also do radio commentaries on NPR. And I've got an upcoming show at the National Academy of Sciences in D.C.. New York street photographs. Come to the opening."

"Of course I will! That's great, Johnny!"

I let his approval sink in.

"I remember your mother's Southern accent," Allen said. "She was from Tennessee, right? A small town with a funny name?"

"Tullahoma."

"That's it! She was very sweet. And strict!"

"I breathed rules."

"I remember." Allen laughed. "And your father was DiMaggio's lawyer. I still tell people that when I was a kid I lived across the street from Joe DiMaggio's lawyer."

I was touched. The last time we saw each other I was a boy with a flat-top who had no idea that my life would become not only *my* past, but also Allen's.

I asked him if his folks were still alive and he told me his mother had died five years ago. His voice dropped a notch and assumed its proper maturity.

I remembered Allen's mother, a small, raven-haired woman with dark, tired eyes. In memory, she stands at the bottom of the stairs in their red house. Her son, who was furious about something, had just run up to his room and slammed the door. She looked at me, a boy who wasn't allowed to slam doors, a boy who was polite to his parents, and shook her head.

I told Allen about my family, my son in high school, my brother's cancer, my folks leaving Sun City and moving to Durham.

It was odd talking to Allen about my parents. As children all we talked about was ourselves—our biceps, our girlfriends, baseball. I tried to picture him as a grown man on the other end of the phone, sitting in a hushed office somewhere above K Street, handsome behind a mahogany desk, surrounded by shelves of leather-bound books, his secretary with white teeth and small glasses sitting on the other side of a glass wall.

"What ever happened to Ellen?" I asked.

Allen laughed. "Do you remember…"

"I know what you're going to say."

We both laughed at the memory of Ellen in her basement, standing beside the washing machine, whipping the towel off and tossing it behind her. Such sad nonchalance as she put one hand behind her head and one on her hip and waggled her torso for five seconds; that shocking tuft of black hair; those enormous breasts and smeared eyes; a fourteen year-old girl in a woman's body performing a striptease for a small crowd of ninth-grade boys who didn't even like her.

Somebody should have been worried about Ellen, that dented girl.

As I talked to Allen, faces came floating up out of those deep waters; teenagers with cracked voices, ponytails and pet peeves.

"Hey, Allen," I asked, "can someone really buy a bank?"

"You can buy anything," Allen said. "Want one? There's one for sale on M Street."

"Not this year."

There was a slight pause in our conversation and then Allen said, "Tell me about Amylu. I heard about it in law school. Did you still know her?"

Allen would remember her, of course, a neighborhood girl, Bob's sister, my girlfriend. I'd forgotten that other people knew her.

"We broke up after I went to prep school, then became friends. I'd see her over vacations. She'd take the Long Island into the city and we'd hang out, see shows, go to museums, that sort of thing."

"How long ago was it?"

I did the math. 1965 to 1990. "Twenty-five years."

"Whoa," Allen said quietly. He went on. "I rarely ran into her after you left. She was what, two years younger than us? I think she hooked up with the artsy crowd in high school."

We paused again, but just for a second.

"Didn't she go to Antioch or somewhere like that?"

"Rhode Island School of Design."

"Right. — How'd she do it? I forgot."

"Drowned herself at Jones Beach." My tone was casual, as if it was an old fact, one among many.

"Right."

"February 1965." I told Allen the story, the bare bones of it. The phone call from RISD to the Danzers. The forced medical-leave. The argument on Jones Beach with her mother. You need help. Amy, stomping off, shouting. "The world is crazy, not me!" Two hours later, no sign of her. The state police, helicopters, no Amy. The bare bones.

"Did Mrs Danzer think she'd killed herself? If she'd been asked to leave school—"

"No, she was just worried about her mental state. She thought there was a good chance Amy had hitched a ride into the city to see me. I was at Columbia, getting a master's degree. Weeks later Amy's body floated up on a beach in Far Rockaway and they identified her through dental records."

We said nothing for a moment.

"So she was pretty screwed up," he said, half a question, half not.

"I guess so," I said.

I didn't say that I occasionally dreamed of her and those dreams always ended in lament.

We talked for a few more minutes, swapping odd little memories of events that were once momentous. Buying firecrackers in the city. Fats Domino at the Brooklyn Paramount. I asked him about Amy's brother, Bob. "Don't know," he said. "I haven't seen him since high school. Last I heard he'd moved to California and dropped out. Designing jewelry, something like that. " Allen laughed at such an improbability. I said, "Wow."

Then he gave me his office number and I said I'd call the next time I was in D.C. and he reminded me that he had a boat, and if I came up this summer, we'd go sailing; I could take lots of beautiful pictures.

"Sounds great," I said.

Allen Raiken and Bob Danzer, 1959

Before we hung up, though, I asked him if he'd ever visited Lake Success after his parents sold their house.

"As a matter of fact, last summer," he said. "On our way to Nantucket I took the kids for a drive around the neighborhood. Still the same, maybe even nicer." He chuckled. "Déjà vu moment coming down Old Farm. There was Mrs Danzer pruning the bushes on her side lawn."

"Mrs Danzer?" I asked.

"Yep."

"Amy's mother?"

"How many Mrs Danzers could I know?"

"I thought they'd moved."

"Why'd you think that?"

"I don't know. After Amy died I thought they'd moved."

"Why would they have moved?"

I paused. "I guess I thought everything would remind them of

Amy, and they'd leave town."

"But they didn't."

"I guess not."

"So you're still a romantic."

"I am? I was?"

"Sure you are," Allen said. "The Danzers moved because everything in the house reminded them of Amy? Only romantics think like that." Suddenly he sounded like a lawyer. "A large colonial on an acre of land, beautiful landscaping, less than half an hour to the city on a good day." He paused. "Anyway, where would they go? You can't escape the death of your child, right?"

He was right about everything.

"Did you stop and say hello?"

"No, I'd made a deal with the kids. No stopping. Do you think I should have?"

I thought he should have.

"No, not necessarily. Anyway, she might not have remembered you."

Allen laughed. "Me, she'd remember. You, that's a different story."

The joke felt good.

"I'm glad you tracked me down, Allen. Great talking to you."

"My pleasure," Allen said. "We'll go out on the boat. I promise. Lots of great photographs. Give me details about the show. Take care, Johnny."

I hung up, feeling almost giddy, as if suspended between my bright Chapel Hill kitchen, and my bedroom at the top of the stairs in Lake Success where, as a teenager, bored with homework and longing for popularity, I'd reshape my pompadour, curl my upper lip, and perform Elvis impersonations in front of the mirror above my dresser.

Hearing Allen's familiar voice had wrenched me back to the 1950s. All those Great Neck kids—had they been standing around in the wings of my memory like a troupe of child actors with funny Long Island accents, waiting for their cue? Ellen. A limping, semi-dangerous boy named Kurtz who wore motorcycle boots and wanted to protect me from enemies I didn't have? A perfect girl named Roberta who always returned from Easter vacation with a dark tan and whose young breasts pressed emphatically against a light lavender sweater? Chucky D, a benign, snuffling boy with freckled milk-white skin and a small, desolate mouth, whose mother had committed suicide when he was in the seventh grade.

But of course it was Amy whose appearance had mattered most of all—at first a backstage shadow, and then, as she quietly approached the light, the girl herself, at home in the world—tall, blond, and quietly observant. And for a few moments there she was again in my sunny kitchen—not the lost young woman whose tragedy I knew perhaps too well, but the happy, uncomplicated girl, a child really, the kind who got goosebumps when I read poems to her.

Yet as quickly as the boys and girls of Great Neck had arrived, conceited, silly, comical, and slightly detached from their carefully crafted personalities, they dissolved like mist into the morning light, leaving me alone with Allen's parting news that the Danzers were still living in Great Neck and presumably could be reached by dialing their old telephone number.

Foolish doesn't begin to describe how I felt. Monumentally foolish. I'd completely forgotten that the Danzers' departure from Great Neck was a story I'd told myself—a fable which I'd come to think of as a fact.

"It doesn't matter who my father was," wrote the poet Anne Sexton, another suicide. "It matters who I remember he was."

But no, it matters who he was.

Later that afternoon, after Allen Raiken's phone call, as I continued to work on the photograph of the gull's shadow (lightening the sand, darkening the shadow), I thought about what I'd say when I talked to Mrs Danzer on the phone. How would she remember me? Warmly? Would she remember that I hadn't sent a condolence card at the time of Amy's death? Perhaps she'd been thinking of other things. Like what do I do with Amy's paintings. Her shoes, her skirts. I'd been guilty of under-imagining. A frivolous man.

I kept working the shadow. Above the shadow was a bird, and the bird had to be imagined.

A dozen prints later I decided to quit working on the photograph of the shadow. I'd spent the better part of the day talking myself into it. I'd imagined an audience standing in a gallery in front of the photograph, touched by its mystery. The gallery walls were white, the floors dark oak. The audience consisted of extremely sensitive people who appreciated the subtlety of my work.

But I couldn't kid myself. The photograph was too precious.

I dumped my chemicals and took my dog Nancy for a walk.

I would contact the Danzers and, together, we would remember their daughter and my friend.

Journal entry, August, 1990

This morning I dream of Amylu, only she isn't in it. In a restaurant I see Mr and Mrs Danzer. He looks young and boyish with his brush mustache, but she looks old, white-haired, kindly. I shake their hands. Her brother Bob is there, looking better than ever, hair more full than ever, darker, softer. I learn they live in Roosevelt. They talk casually about things that don't interest me. I want to ask them about their photograph albums so badly that even the prospect of seeing the albums makes me feel as if I will cry. At some point, Allen Raiken comes over to the table and Bob puts an entire branch, leaves and all, in his mouth, as if he is eating an hors d'oeuvre. I guess I never ask my question because at the end of the dream I am turning the pages of a phone book which covers all Long Island and I am looking under D for Amylu's number in case her folks don't know she is alive.

LIGHT PASSING THROUGH LEAVES: VISITING THE DANZERS

Photographs console us in the face of death and oblivion - it's their fundamental gift; they testify to what has been and what will be no more, and this testimony matters. It matters because oblivion is actually more than we can handle; because we get old and lose faith in the quick and competent gods of our childhood; because, unless we deny what our eyes see or turn ourselves into machinery, the future of everything is full of loss and disappearing; because we not only forget but we're also forgotten.

John Rosenthal

"Mulberry Street: The Story of a Photograph," *Five Points*

The moment she answered the phone and said, "Helen Danzer," I remembered her brusque telephone manner. And when I introduced myself as "a voice from the past," she said, after a small pause, "Well, now that's a surprise," but she didn't sound surprised.

I was a little nervous. The last time we'd spoken was in Great Neck, in the Danzers' living room, on a cold Friday morning in February, 1965, two days after Amylu disappeared from Jones Beach. She'd hoped that, as Amy's oldest friend, I could shed some light on her disappearance. I couldn't.

Twenty-five years later I was afraid Mrs Danzer was going to ask me point-blank why I was calling, but instead she asked me questions about my life—where did I live? did I have a family? had I finished my degree at Columbia? was I now Dr Rosenthal?—and then, after I skated across a few brief answers, she invited me to drive out to Great Neck the next day. "We'll take advantage of this nice weather," she said warmly, "and have lunch on the screen porch. Bob will be happy to see you. There's a lot of catching up to do."

"I'd love to," I said, though I wondered if Bob would be glad to see me. I never liked him and I don't think he liked me.

"You remember where we live?" Mrs Danzer asked lightly.

I laughed. "Nineteen Fox Hunt Lane, the house on the corner." Remember where Amylu had lived?

After I hung up I thought, maybe after lunch the Danzers will show me photographs. They must have photographs of Amy. I didn't. Not a single one.

I pictured Amy standing on the slate steps in front of her house, her hands gawky at the end of her arms—Amy, captured with a sharp lens and good film, preserved in silvery brilliance for the years.

A photograph.

That half-light in which the dead appear, saying, *Back again*.

The next morning I rented a car and left the city around 11:30. It was my first trip to Great Neck in decades—not since the morning I'd sat with Mrs Danzer in her dark living room and we'd pretended Amy was still alive.

Driving through the Midtown Tunnel and onto the Long Island Expressway I recalled those early teenage years (I was probably around fourteen) when I'd fallen in love with the Danzers' tall, excitable thirteen-year-old daughter. She was the perfect girlfriend for a boy like me—a shorty who wanted to impress girls. She'd listen quietly as I made distinctions between "us" and "them": they played bridge, we didn't; they listened to moonlight favorites by the Percy Faith Orchestra, we didn't.

When Amy's grades had plummeted the Danzers restricted our telephone calls to ten minutes. And once a furious Mr Danzer had banned me from the house after he'd discovered—before I told Amy where I'd put it—an effusive love note stuffed between two rocks in the garden wall. Amy, he told me angrily, was too young for that sort of thing. Did I understand? Yes, I did.

Exits with familiar names swept by: Corona, Elmhurst, Kissena Boulevard, Ozone Park. The monoliths of LeFrak City towered above the flat Queens landscape.

Passing Marathon Parkway, I recalled that during her sophomore year at RISD, Amy and her father had quarreled over the courses she was taking. She wanted to major in Painting; he insisted on Graphic Design. "You're living in a dreamworld!" Mr Danzer had shouted. "You can paint in your spare time! You need to be practical!" (Mr Danzer, as I recalled, worked on Madison Avenue, designing ads for Domino Sugar, an occupation which, at the time, seemed vaguely immoral to me.) "I'm not going to sell out," Amy had shouted back.

But that didn't sound like Amy at all; it sounded like me.

What did I actually remember?

I was sure about "dreamworld."

No, I wasn't.

"Selling out," I thought, as I took the exit to Lake Success. The great Shalt Not of my twenties. Now, post-Warhol, merely a quaint notion.

Things mattered to Amy: Jackson Pollock, Siddhartha, Joan Baez, driftwood, "Red River Valley," falling snow, *The L-Shaped Room*. A lovely, spare constellation of mid-century enchantments.

Friends who'd never met Amy said that she'd killed herself because she was mentally ill, probably schizophrenic. As years went by, "bipolar" was added to the list. You could add anything to the list. Depression. My mother didn't believe in mental illness; she believed in strength of character; you could always pull yourself together. Amy didn't. Everyone had an interpretation of Amylu's death, even though there was no diagnosis. A note would have helped, *anything*, but she left nothing.

What had been known, observed?

She "walked around in a daze." Stared at her painting for hours

104

at a time. Read Camus. Kept her coat on in all weathers. Stopped talking. Wrote an essay just before her death complaining about dorm life. Not enough. Not enough.

Why did she do it?

I pulled off on Horace Harding and turned left on Old Farm Road and there was the Danzers' house, on the corner of Meadow Woods and Fox Hunt Lane, larger than I remembered, and deeply-shaded.

I began to prepare for the role I was about to play—that of a friendly middle-aged man paying a social call to the parents of his childhood friend. I hoped that my smiles and (feigned) interest in their lives would lead us back to the 1950s—to a conversation about Amy, and, of course, to the photographs. I could revisit the details of her face and talk about her, finally.

Don't forget, I told myself, this is supposed to be a social call, not a fishing expedition.

Glancing up the block, I saw, in the soft light of late morning, that all of the houses were larger than I remembered, their lawns disconcertingly green. Nothing disturbed the eye—no dogs, no unpruned bushes, no bright toys on grass. The driveways looked scrubbed.

At prep school, influenced by city boys who were hipper than I was, I'd learned to despise the suburbs. I'd say things like "You have to be insane to live in the suburbs." And yet, as I turned right into the Danzer's driveway, I thought: Insane? It's beautiful here.

Mrs Danzer was picking up twigs on a slope of lawn under the large oak tree. She wore white tennis sneakers and a baggy work sweater. A denim visor shaded her face. As I pulled into the driveway she added the twigs in her hand to a small pile by a hedge, and walked slowly across the yard. I wondered if she was thinking about the last time we saw each other.

Wearing a warm smile, she put her hand out and I shook it. I said, "It's so nice to see you, Mrs Danzer," and she said, "Please, call me Helen. How long has it been?"

"Decades."

"Are you still a Johnny or have you become a John?"

"John, I guess. My son's the Johnny now."

"You'll have to tell me about him."

Helen Danzer was a little smaller than I remembered, a little wider. She appeared to be a vigorous older woman at home in the outdoors, by no means diminished—as I had once imagined—by the long-ago suicide of her daughter. She looked at me curiously, even whimsically, her brown eyes comically magnified by the thick lenses of her glasses. When I'd lived in Great Neck I assumed that every mother should be as charming and graceful as mine, with a sweet laugh that made everybody happy. I hadn't liked Mrs Danzer, who, unlike my mother, wasn't charming.

I followed her inside. Over the years I'd returned to the Danzer house in my dreams—bewildering dreams, always. Once I dreamed of a tremulous young woman in a print dress sitting on the edge of Amy's bed, a woman who'd just returned to life but couldn't remain long. In another dream, Amy, wearing modern clothing (jeans and running shoes) told me she'd never committed suicide; her death had been staged for reasons she was about to explain to me when I woke up.

I glanced to my left in the foyer at the stairway leading up to Amy's room.

The living-room furniture was arranged more or less as I remembered it—a large couch still faced the back yard with its terraced garden. Here Amy and I had danced to Little Richard and Bill Haley and the Comets, and once, when her mother was out shopping and her brother was playing basketball across the street, we lay on the couch and kissed and I sang the lyrics to "Party Doll" into her ear. Blond hair, eyes of blue, gonna have a party with you. From my young heart to hers.

I followed Helen to the screen porch. On a round wicker table our lunch sat under plastic wrap.

"Just before I left Great Neck after ninth grade," I said brightly, "Amy held a surprise party for me out here." "That's nice." Helen re-

106

plied and smiled. Then she looked down at the lunch she'd prepared. I could make out tuna or chicken salad, crusty French bread, sliced tomatoes. "Robert's going to join us," she said. "He should be here soon. Make yourself at home. I made some ice tea this morning. Is that okay?" Sure, I said, and she headed for the kitchen.

In the 1950s, a few blocks away on Birch Hill Road, my mother held Canasta luncheons on our screen-porch. Pimento cheese canapés, deviled eggs, fruit floating in Jell-O. Walking home after the school bus had dropped me off, I'd hear the laughter of women drifting on blue smoke above my mother's rhododendrons.

Across Meadow Woods a sprinkler tossed radiant bands of water onto the left side of the Calhouns' lawn. Larry Calhoun, I recalled, was a year or two older than me, a chilly boy with a squarish head, a neat little hair-do and a startlingly filthy mind. One day in his basement he showed me his father's hidden stash of small, soiled, black-and-white comic books. I still remembered the first one he showed me: Archie and Jughead fucking Betty and Veronica, Jughead's dick a foot long, and Betty, in a balloon above her head, shrieking with pleasure. Shocked and excited, I'd pretended otherwise. "These are really funny," I said, trying to catch my breath.

Amy and I had spent hours on this porch.

I'd imagined her last day many times: a bright-blue cold February day; the ocean roaring; her mother, a beach away, sketching, fuming; a cliff of still white clouds off to the south. And then, just like that— walking, inconceivably, into the ocean? Into waves? What happened then? A moment of indecision? The weight of winter clothes?

Futile to ask.

When Helen returned to the porch with a pitcher of ice tea, she smiled at me and I smiled back, happy because the gap between her front teeth was familiar.

As we waited for Mr Danzer, Helen asked me what I liked to photograph. I told her that for almost twenty years I'd been photographing the city itself, its streets, parks, subways, and museums. But not just the city—the disappearing city—certain places and things and even landscapes that seemed vulnerable to me, that seemed almost like relics of a bygone era. "Some of them are already gone," I said. "A Jewish bakery on East 7th Street, an Italian sailor's club on Mulberry Street. I've never thought of myself as a documentary photographer, but I ended up documenting things that people are starting to miss." As I spoke, I felt that I was not only addressing Mrs Danzer, but also her daughter, an almost visible young presence.

A cargo van pulled into the driveway and a few seconds later Mr Danzer practically bounded onto the porch. At least I assumed it was Mr Danzer. I remembered Amy's father as a rigid, peevish, impatient, dislikable, pale man with a bristly moustache, a Methodist, who, on most evenings, worked over a drafting table in a small office off the living-room. Everyone tiptoed around his moods. This man was short, ebullient, friendly, clean-shaven, and wore red suspenders. His eyes were fox-bright, and he shook my hand with a quick, outdoor grip. "Robert Danzer," he said vigorously, as if we'd never met. Immediately he began to complain about job-site problems. The hydraulic system of a rented front-loader. "Two hours lost. Goddamned incompetence. I'm starving," he said. "What have you been up to these years? Helen tells me you're a photographer. Bob's a massage therapist in Monterey. Started out in engineering, switched to jewelry, and now massage. Massage therapy!" He laughed as he poured me a glass of ice tea. "Something in the air out there!"

Allen Raiken had told me that he'd heard Bob had "dropped out," but he didn't know more than that. "A massage therapist," I said, surprised. "I wouldn't have guessed."

"Can't make up his mind. Not with women either. Been married three times. Can't keep it zipped." Robert gave me a quick wink. "How long has it been since you've been in touch with Bob?"

Bob and I had never been in touch. Not since I'd left Great Neck at fifteen. When I lived in the neighborhood I'd come over and we'd hang out, but I was really there to see his younger sister, who irritated him. Bob was into cars and talked a lot about four-barrel carbs and rack and pinion steering.

A massage therapist. Well, good for him.

108

The Danzers, however, seemed to believe that Bob and I had been great friends and that I was eager to hear about his life—that hearing about his life was the point of this visit. During lunch they told me—occasionally talking over each other—about Bob's wives and his two children. The photographs of Bob surprised me. Once a stocky, impudent boy with gingery hair, Bob had transformed into a handsome man with styled silvery hair and a laid-back smile. Then more photographs showed up—overexposed instamatics of the Long Island landscapes Mr Danzer had designed. A sunken terraced garden on an estate once owned by the Vanderbilts. A Japanese rock garden in Kings Point with tumbling water.

All conversational routes to Amy appeared to be closed.

Why?

"Do you remember our rock garden in the back of the house?" Helen asked me. But she answered her own question. "Well of course you don't. Who pays attention to gardens at that age?" She tossed off an easy laugh. "The children never did."

"The children." Amy, finally.

But I did remember the garden—an out-of-bounds place behind the house with large and small flowers, boulders, vines, trickling water, little paths, a tree trunk chiseled out for planting; I recalled carefully extracting a baseball from flattened violets. I also remembered biking over to the Danzers' one afternoon and finding Bob and Larry Calhoun running around like monkeys under a tree that leaned over the rock garden. They were shouting "On the rag, on the rag!" and as I came around the corner of the garage, Bob saw me, and, howling with laughter, pointed to one of the lower branches. A sanitary belt draped down like viscera. Amy, looking out of her bedroom window, her face distorted, was screaming like a wounded creature.

Parents are blind.

Robert told me they'd landscaped their first garden in 1945. He spoke about its flowers and shrubs as others might speak about the children they raised, praising the beauty of the snow azaleas and the layered and domed Japanese maple.

Helen said, "Before you leave, I'll give you the tour. The camellias are just coming in."

"I'd like that," I replied politely.

Had I played my role too well?

Later, after lunch was over and Robert had gone back to work, Mrs Danzer and I remained on the porch sipping tea. The afternoon was turning a little muggy. We talked about the old neighborhood— who had left, who remained.

I couldn't imagine anything worse than this pleasant conversation.

I wanted to say, *"Don't you remember that on the day that Amy disappeared you thought she might have hitch-hiked into the city to find me? That I was her best friend?"*

"Would you mind if we talked a little about Amylu?" I asked. "It's been a long time since I've talked to anyone who knew her."

Helen looked closely at her glass of tea as she placed it slowly on the table. She kept her eyes on the glass and said slowly, without intonation, "Well, I won't pretend there's a part of me that doesn't ache."

A young woman in a baseball cap walked down Old Farm Road as a bright yellow school bus, its brakes squealing, pulled up in front of the Calhouns' driveway. The bus doors opened and a pale, little girl, holding the rail, stood on the bottom step, bent her knees, and jumped onto the curb, her pink backpack bouncing above her thin shoulders. Whirling around, she waved her tiny hands and shouted goodbyes to her friends, whose wild little faces peered behind the glass of half-opened windows. "Good bye, Madison! Bye Timmy!" The bus drove off, its roaring engine drowning out the racket of kids out of school.

Helen's statement had taken me by surprise. I'd failed to imagine the long reach of grief.

For a second, I was tempted to say "I understand," letting us go on with the polite conversation we'd been having up till then. But I didn't. Instead, I said gently, "Do you have any photographs of Amylu you could show me? Even a snapshot?"

After a pause Helen said, "Why would you want to see a picture of Amylu?"

"Why?"

"Yes, why do you want to see a picture of her?"

A picture. A photograph. In my world the distinction was important. It wasn't now.

Was there a note of hostility in Helen's question? Probably not. But the question was deep. Was I a serious man, or a light-hearted man poking around? It was nice that I'd called and dropped by, but why would niceness entitle me to anything but a tuna salad sandwich? Amylu had been dead for twenty-five years: why now this desire to see her photograph? Didn't I have pictures of my own? Or did Helen mean that photographs aren't merely ordinary household objects we take for granted—they can lacerate you, punish you, leave you sleepless, and, hidden away in a drawer, they shouldn't be disturbed.

I didn't answer her immediately. Then I said, "I don't know." A blue jay jeered in the near distance. "I don't have a single photograph of Amylu." I paused for a second, then went on. "When she was thirteen she said to me, 'You're sensitive, you don't have to act like the other boys.' I've never forgotten that." I laughed. "It might have changed my life." Helen was looking at me intently, her eyes, magnified behind her glasses, partly obscured by reflected sunlight. "All I have of Amy is a silly postcard she sent me from Bear Mountain when she was thirteen. That's it. I'd love to see a photograph of her. Even one. I think of her a lot. Sometimes I dream about her."

Helen looked off and said casually, "Well, there's a few around here some place. Maybe in the hall closet. I always meant to put them in an album. It may take a while to find them."

I pushed my luck.

"Do you have any of Amy's paintings. I've never seen one."

"Oh, Lord," Helen said with a laugh. "Somewhere. Somewhere in the basement, I'm sure. With all my unsold paintings. You don't want to go down there. It's a mess."

A painting: it would be Amy herself.

111

"I really do. And I'd love to see your work."

At the bottom of the basement stairs I paused, startled. Banks of fluorescent lights clicked on. Once a dreary storage space, the basement was as bright as a beach. The ping-pong table was gone. So, too, the smell of mold and cold cement. Something different now.

"Linseed oil," Helen said as if she could read my mind. "I use it to thin oils. It takes longer to dry, but I'm in no hurry. I go back and forth between oils and acrylics."

The basement, shadowless, held its original symmetry. A memory arrived: Amylu sitting on the ping-pong table, saying "Charlie Salvator asked me to go to the movies and I said yes." My heart had practically stopped beating and I'd thought, That's impossible, we have a song, you can't go to the movies with Charlie Salvator if we have a song.

Now, stacked according to size, rows of framed canvases reached, like small waves, three or four feet into the room. Two unfinished landscapes sat on easels.

I thought: On that Sunday in February they drove to Providence and went to Amy's dorm room and told her they were taking her home, and she said (for apparently she'd started talking again), there's a mistake, you're making a big mistake, you need to talk to my psychologist, he knows what's going on. And her parents replied, "Amy, he's the one who called us. He said you needed counseling they couldn't provide." And loading her clothes and paintings into their station wagon, they'd driven her, a grim, dumbfounded young woman, back to Long Island. Did she sit in the front seat with her father, staring silently out the window? Did she weep in the backseat, wondering if she should end her life?

I thought, Amy's paintings are down here somewhere.

Helen was touched by my eagerness to look at her work. She showed me old oils, newer acrylics, watercolors, flowers of all sorts, trees, brooks, ocean. "After all these years I've finally learned to control watercolors," she said, holding a small painting before her. "Their transparency allows me to create the impression of light passing through leaves."

112

Then Helen spotted a dusty painting lying on a shelf above her canvases.

"Oh, here's one."

She brushed it with a small towel and laid it against a wall, stepping back, and I knelt in front of it.

Ten seconds passed.

"It's very youthful," Helen said. "Remember, she was only a second year studio student."

It was a poorly executed oil painting. A couple of figures in the midst of wild brushstrokes and a jagged color palette. A student's painting. She'd been young. Somehow I'd forgotten that. A novice. Her skills left to the future.

I said nothing. I didn't know what I had expected.

"I always thought Amy's talent was in her drawings," Mrs Danzer said. "A natural. Some of her drawings reminded me of Da Vinci. I'm not exaggerating. Her attention to detail. But she didn't respect that particular talent. Not enough anyway. Thought of it as illustration. She was struggling. I suppose she wanted to be the next de Kooning or Pollock." Helen was looking at Amy's stillborn painting. "She always tuned out what she didn't want to hear."

"Do you have any of her drawings?"

"Somewhere. I don't know where." Helen paused. "When it happened I sent a few to some of the girls she knew at college."

Mrs Danzer picked up Amy's painting, studied it for a few seconds, and put it back on the shelf.

Sitting on the porch again, Helen rummaged through a manila envelope. At one point she turned to me. "What am I looking for?" Before I could answer she said, "Oh yes, photos of Bob and Amy. They're in here somewhere—hang on."

"Was Amy wearing a red dress on the day of her confirmation?"

Helen looked up at me quizzically and then turned away.

"No, she wore a white dress with a red sash," she said evenly.

"She looked beautiful, didn't she?"

Helen nodded her head and smiled "Yes, she looked beautiful."

A thirteen-year old with long blond hair falling across her shoulders, standing in a line with seven or eight other girls wearing inter-changeable white dresses. One red sash.

She pulled out a few photographs of young children. "Oh, my," Helen said. I looked at them briefly. Then she handed me a pho-tograph. "She must have been twelve or thirteen in that one." A bleached Polaroid of Amy leaning against a 1957 Pontiac station wagon, obviously bored. "Look at her, making a face." I remem-bered the car and the girl. Helen chuckled, "Look at that lipstick," she said, handing me another one, this one of Amy standing beside a tree, posing for the camera, her lips red as blood. "Oh, here's her senior picture," she said, studying the photograph before she passed it on to me. A wallet-sized, black-and-white, head-and-shoulders studio portrait—pearls, satin prom dress, bare shoulders, skin like milk. I was touched; I'd never seen a glamorous Amy, an Amy who'd cared about her appearance. "That's some hair-do," I said and Helen laughed. "It's called a flip. Jackie Kennedy made it famous. Amy hat-ed it. The fights we had." She reached over and took the photograph from my hand, turning it over. Then, without a word, she handed it to me. On the back was written, in a familiar handwriting: "How mellowed and sweet these trying years will seem when time erases all petty aspirations and useless tensions: you're always mom, Love Amylu."

I had to ask the question. If I left without asking it, I'd never forgive myself.

"Why did she do it?" I asked.

Helen paused, but only for a second. "I don't know the answer to that. I wish I did." She looked at the small pile of photographs on the table. "She became silent. They sent her home when she be-gan to sit in the halls saying nothing. There were other things but I can't remember them now. All of us were very confused. She wasn't well and needed help, but we didn't get it in time."

She looked away and sighed.

"Time has a way of softening the blows that life gives us," she said.

I said nothing. There was nothing to say.

114

After a pause she said lightly, "Why don't you keep this?" and she held out Amy's graduation photograph.

I looked at it, mid-air.

"I couldn't do that."

"Don't you want it?"

"Sure, but it's yours. And Bob might want it."

"He's not sentimental. And I have a big one upstairs."

"In that case, yes, thanks."

After a quick tour of the garden, we chatted for a few more minutes in the driveway. I felt like I'd been on a long journey and she looked tired. I thanked her for the lunch and for the private exhibition. She laughed it off and we shook hands. "Next time," she said, "bring your photographs. I'll count on it." As I got into the car, I asked her if she still drove into the city. "Occasionally, she said, "not often." Then she looked at me in a nameless sort of way and said, "Every time I take the Triborough Bridge into Manhattan, I look over at the asylum on Ward Island and think that if Amy had lived she might have spent her entire life behind one of those barred windows. She'd be forty-six now. Or forty-seven." Helen smiled and patted my arm on the window ledge. "It was good to see you, Johnny." Catching herself, she laughed. "John, I mean." she said. "Come back." There was a mist in her eyes.

I nodded my head, started the car, and left.

A few minutes later, as I turned onto the Long Island Expressway, I began to cry. I cried for Mrs Danzer who had to choose between an Amylu who committed suicide or an Amylu staring vacantly out of a barred window. At what bitter depth does such a choice exist? And I cried for my own insufficiencies, my glibness, my failure to send a condolence note or to imagine Amy's death from any angle but my own—and I cried because only a few hours ago I'd been ready to engage the Danzers in a nostalgic romp through their daughter's brief life.

I shouldn't have come, I thought. I shouldn't have presumed. One can't just slip into peoples' lives with a secret curiosity and con them with smiles. I wondered if the Danzers had dreaded the prospect of my visit. Had they prepared their own concealments? I should have realized that my visit could only reopen a wound Time and oblivion had done its best to heal. I was, after all, her first love and last friend.

It was all so complicated. Amy had come to me in dreams over which I had no control. The "why" of her death had become, accidentally, the archetypal mystery of my life. Who was she? What happened? Did she matter? What do we remember? Who does the remembering? What does mental illness mean? Why suicide?

I wondered what Helen—Mrs Danzer—was doing now. Was she adding to her pile of twigs? Was she sitting on the porch, motionless, looking at old photographs?

During a brief traffic jam near Utopia Parkway I picked up the photograph of Amy and looked at it closely. She'd never looked so dolled-up, so not-Amy. It didn't matter. Like a film spooling backwards, the little photograph reversed the dispersions of death and brought together the scattered memory of eyes, skin, teeth, forehead—the vaguely lost coherency of my friend, which, for a moment or two, challenged death, and won. She was beside me in the car. She wasn't dead.

Oh, photographs.

Then she was dead.

WARD ISLAND

The parting image that Helen had left me with, that of Amylu staring dully out of a barred window at passing cars, stayed with me for a few days. I'd never imagined what sort of life Amylu might actually have lived if she'd survived her suicide attempt, or changed her mind at the last moment. Nor did I question the validity of the image, or distrust its sadness. If one accepted the premise of Amylu's mental illness, it was only logical to imagine her confined—and why not the asylum on Wards Island? As a boy I'd stare nervously at the huge, drab, multi-winged complex whenever my folks would drive across the Triborough Bridge into Manhattan. Everybody knew it was the insane asylum. To kids it was a famously creepy place. "Those poor lost souls," my mother had said more than once as we drove by.

It's possible that Helen was afraid that if Amylu had lived she might have become one of those agitated patients who refuses treatment and shouts things like, "The world is crazy, not me!"—her final, desperate (and curious) words on the beach. Helen wouldn't have been alone in assuming that the medical response to such wild behavior was sedation. Popular magazines like *Life* had published stories and photographs that documented the terrible conditions inside state mental hospitals, with photographs of listless, over-medicated patients wandering around, sitting in chairs, looking at the floor or staring vacantly out of barred windows. In such a place, Helen thought, Amylu "might have spent her entire life."

Yet even if it had turned out that Amylu was suffering from a

118

definable mental illness, which was never proven to be the case, the mental image of Amylu behind a barred window was, in the 1990s, more cinematic than realistic. Times had changed—slowly at first, but then more rapidly. In the mid-1960s, a broad critique of inhumane institutional psychiatry—influenced, to some extent, by the public's shocked reaction to Ken Kesey's 1962 novel *One Flew Over the Cuckoo's Nest*—was taking place. And a new generation of psychotropic drugs—and then a second generation in the 1980s—allowed many mentally ill patients to function normally, or if not normally, then at least outside of barred windows. The image of Amylu staring out of a window on Ward Island, her sense of the world around her muffled by Thorazine, was based on a therapeutic model that was already obsolete in the 1990s. In fact, if Amylu had survived her crisis in 1965, she might have been treated in Great Neck while living in her upstairs bedroom above the rock garden. A careful, leveled life, but still, a life with, maybe, enough joy to balance sorrow.

Of course Helen's parting remark was wholly speculative. Yes, Amy might have been mentally ill and required some sort of confinement, but it's no less conceivable that she would have responded well to therapy or recovered her balance quite naturally, after which she might have resumed her studies at RISD and gone on to lead a normal life. However, there is little consolation to be had from thinking about these alternative outcomes, since they raise the tragic possibility that Amylu's suicide wasn't just the result of misery, but of misery coupled with youthful impatience. In that case, her suicide could be viewed as a terrible mistake, which is an intolerable thought.

CARMEL, CALIFORNIA: BOB

Dressed in loose linen trousers and a bright Hawaiian shirt, handsomer than I remembered, Bob barely resembled the boisterous boy from Lake Success, a boy obsessed with cars—in particular the 1956 cherry-red Chevy with wrap-around windows. His hair, once shaped into a tense flat-top, was graying and wavy. To my delight, he kept shape-shifting across the table from me—from the restless boy to the easygoing and collected California man. I was tempted to lean across the table and say, in the old language, "Hey, Bob, cut the shit. You can't fool me."

The small gap between his two front teeth was exactly like his mother's, and I found that touching.

The café was charming. Striped awnings and whitewashed adobe walls; sunlight streaming in through large arched windows. Around us, tanned, handsome people sat at little marble-top tables drinking coffee. A young boy, sitting by the window with his father, picked the glaze off his pastry. Behind Bob, two middle-aged women in tennis skirts, sunglasses perched on their heads, laughed melodiously and drank white wine.

I'd driven down to Carmel from San Francisco where my wife and I were staying with friends. After my visit with the Danzers in Great Neck, I'd grown curious about Bob. What were his thoughts, after all these years, regarding his sister's suicide? What had his reaction been when he'd heard she was missing? His mother had told me that Bob wasn't sentimental about the past, but what did that mean? That he was one of those forward-looking people who keep their eye on the future—or one of those people for whom the past barely exists? If the latter, I'd be out of luck.

I remembered Bob as a boy with a bad temper. Once, when his mother told him to mow the lawn, he'd slammed his fist against the kitchen wall. He quarreled with his sister a lot, but they must have worked something out over the years. The last time I saw Amylu she'd just returned from visiting Bob in the Midwest.

For about half an hour our conversation meandered through Lake Success in the late 1950s—my junior high school years. I wanted to know what had happened to some of the kids, the serious athletes, the beautiful girls, the nerds, the rich kids whose parents bought them a car when they turned sixteen. In retrospect, I did most of the talking and asked all of the questions. Bob smiled now and then when I reminded him of our young obsessions— the 1957 Yankees, Fats Domino at the Brooklyn Paramount Theater—even the way we'd shout out the lyrics to a Coasters song, "Stranded in the Jungle." But he wasn't really there—not in the playful way I was. For a moment, I even wondered if he quite remembered me. After all, I'd left Lake Success in the ninth grade, just as he was about to embark on the much more memorable days of high school.

A few minutes later, when I stopped trying to stir up old memories, I asked Bob why he ended up in California instead of New York. His answer, which I'm recalling at a distance of decades, was quiet and yet not without passion; it caught me off-guard. The East Coast, he said, was unlivable, its skies polluted, its karma heavy; its cancer rates were high. Easterners, he said, did their thing, but it was an old thing, an obsolete thing; here, on the West Coast, people were less negative, less judgmental, more open to change and right brain intuition. (Later, I would recall Walker Percy's description of a woman at a western dude ranch who still carried with her "the old civil sorrowful air of the East.") He talked about yoga and meditation, and therapeutic massage—anything that could reduce stress and help one live in the present moment.

I was surprised by Bob's self-transformation. I had assumed that the man I was meeting for a chat would be just an older version of the

121

obstinate and often angry Bob I knew in 1958. But the man in front of me was almost comically not-Bob, and I liked this man better.

I also understood why he lacked sentiment for the past.

He was an escapee.

And why not? And why not here, where Moroccan coffee and bright colors and Vivaldi's "Spring"—lightly, quietly, distinctly—defied the old strictures, the old mess?

Bob asked me if I had any interest in photographing Big Sur, a landscape he loved. It was a good question and it reminded me that Robinson Jeffers, a poet I'd read in college, had lived in Carmel in a rock cottage by the sea. An angry man, he'd mourned, in fierce lines, the destruction of wild places, the approach of the suburbs. A photograph came to mind—Jeffers brooding on a rocky outcrop, the Pacific seething behind him.

I leaned across the table, and quietly, beneath the hum of conversation and laughter, I said to Bob, "What are your thoughts about your sister's suicide? I'm thinking about writing a book about her."

Bob didn't pause. He'd probably been waiting. "I'm not sure she committed suicide."

"What do you mean?"

In dreams Amy had told me that her death had been a ruse.

"She might have been murdered."

Such a possibility had crossed my mind, of course, but it never quite added up—all it offered was an excuse not to think about the problem of Amylu.

"How many killers hang out on Jones Beach in February?"

"Or a rapist," Bob said, "who covered his tracks by drowning her. There's no evidence she committed suicide."

"She wasn't herself. RISD sent her home. They must have had a reason."

"She was depressed," Bob said, "but that doesn't mean she wanted to kill herself."

"No, I suppose not."

This is what I'd been waiting for, this dark turn in our conversation. I was here in Carmel to transport Bob back—away from this sunlight and soft music and clinking cutlery—to the gray coast and the pale girl.

I said, "Amy and your mother had an argument on the beach and Amy stormed off. Do you know if she had her sketch pad with her? Was it ever found?"

A shadow of irritation passed across Bob's features. The question, even as I asked it, seemed peculiar, a little off-center, a cop's question.

"I don't remember much about Amylu's disappearance," he said matter-of-factly. "I wasn't there. I'd just started a new job with John Deere in Iowa and I couldn't get away."

My younger self might have said, "Your sister was missing and you couldn't get away?" But that younger self didn't exist anymore. I thought instead: Amy was missing. That's all any of us knew. Why would Bob get on a plane and fly back to Long Island when Amylu could have reappeared at any moment? It was his first job after college.

Then Bob added, "And my parents didn't want to talk about it."

"I understand," I said, even though I didn't.

There was a long pause. Then I said, "Sorry to be such a downer, Bob. I just wondered what it must have been like when Amy first disappeared."

Bob sipped his coffee. "I don't know. I was in Iowa."

The barista, a young bearded man wearing a hairnet, moved like a dancer between small gleaming machines. Behind Bob, the middle-aged tennis players, into their second glass, laughed continuously. Pretty people. Coastal paradise.

I pushed my cup and saucer away from me. It was time to head back to San Francisco.

This time Bob leaned across the table.

"It's possible she walked into the ocean like Siddhartha walked into the river."

Siddhartha, I thought, as Bob's words hung in the air, already making a dippy kind of sense. Amylu and Siddhartha. The young despairing man and the river. The beauty of flowing water. Om. Perfection

"She was very into Hesse's book before she died," Bob said. "In

123

high school she learned calligraphy and copied a chapter from *Sid-dhartha* into a book she'd made by hand. She may have wanted to cleanse herself and be reborn."

I remembered her telling me about the book. Rice paper.

It's possible, I thought—a miscalculation; February ocean, hypo-thermia.

But Siddhartha didn't walk into the river. Nor did he die.

Still, as I paid our bill at the counter, I took momentary comfort in the thought of Amy being reborn.

Outside, Bob asked me to walk with him to his office a couple of blocks away. The woman he was living with was going to drop a package off at his studio, and he'd like me to meet her. As we crossed a bright parking lot, a youngish blond woman pulled up in a small car, smiling. She wound down her window and handed Bob a small package. He introduced us and I shook her hand. She was wearing sunglasses like a movie star in disguise. The midday sun, reflected in both green lenses, rose higher as she leaned my way. For a fraction of a second I thought it was Amylu. Lips, smile, teeth. Startling—then gone. A trick of light. "I understand you two go way back," she said sweetly. Her handshake lingered, as if I were a person who mattered, a relative perhaps. "Too far," I said, as if Bob and I were already old men with a grand history of friendship.

Driving back to San Francisco, I wondered if Bob had actually made a clean break with the past.

I haven't seen him since, though we have had intermittent email exchanges in more recent years. In 2016, at my request, he sent me copies of a few photographs of Amylu that he'd inherited from his parents. We became "friends" on Facebook where he occasionally posts inspiring quotations that extol love, compassion, and forgive-ness. The year before, on February 24, 2015, I sent him an email noting the fiftieth anniversary of his sister's death. He replied im-mediately, saying that probably explained why he'd felt her pres-ence lately.

SIDDHARTHA

Helen Danzer and I kept in touch. I'd send her an announcement of a new exhibit of my photographs to which she'd respond with a sweet, laudatory note. At Christmas time she'd send me a card with news of Bob's family. Once or twice she commented on her increasing frailty. Then one day UPS delivered a package that contained a thin, journal-sized book with an almost translucent rice-paper cover. Hand-made; obviously fragile, the faint whiff of mold. As if I were touching a wound, I timidly opened the book. A card inside from Helen: "I was cleaning out a closet today and came across Amylu's senior art project in high school. I know you cared about her so I thought it might find a home with you. I don't remember why she chose this particular book to transcribe. She had a mind of her own. It sure took me back! Warmly, Helen."

The book was bound with white thread and on the title page was written:

By The River – from Siddhartha
By Herman Hesse
Transcribed and Selected by
Amylu Danzer

I sat down and turned a few pages. Meticulous gothic calligraphy marched evenly across textured watercolor paper; small paintings, mosaic-like, radiant, appeared here and there—so, too, faintly, the almost indiscernible creep of mildew. A tiny painting fell from its old, honey-colored glue and I caught it between my knees: a cardboard bird—Siddhartha's heart that no longer sang. As I read, I remembered the despairing young Siddhartha who'd been corrupted by city life and had become nauseated by his own existence. I remembered how he'd clung to a coconut tree and stared into the fierce, chill water of a woodland river. What had restrained him, saved him, returned him to sleep? Yes, of course, a sacred word—OM—its resonant sound welling up within the lost soul. I read the words, and wondered why Amy had chosen this particular moment to transcribe and illustrate the passage? Had she longed, at seventeen, for some sort of restoration?

Or was it merely that as a young artist she'd wanted to submerge herself into the novel's flourishing green landscape?

As I read Amy's Siddhartha, a different story began to compete with Hesse's immaculate voice. It was the story of a young woman standing on the coast of an injured country, looking intently at the sea. The sky is blue, but it's dirty; the day is cold, but she's not aware of it. Like Siddhartha, she is unhappy, fearful, sleepless, and lost. The words that once expressed her spirit—family, love, art, God—mean nothing to her. For her, the possibility of refreshing sleep doesn't exist—she is stuck in her misery without points of light. At that moment, in this story, the only certainty is the rhythm of the large, roaring waves piling on top of each other, and she walks into them. They are voiceless. There is no restoration.

I told myself this story as I read Amy's transcription of Siddhartha's sweet survival.

little so that he could fall headlong and finally go under. He bent, with closed eyes — towards death.

Then from a remote part of his soul, from the past of his tired life, he heard a sound. It was one word, one syllable, which without thinking he spoke indistinctly, the ancient beginning and ending of all Brahman prayers, the holy Om, which had the meaning of "the Perfect one" or "Perfection". At that moment, when the sound of Om reached his ears, his slumbering soul suddenly awakened and he recognized the folly of his action.

Siddartha was deeply horrified. So that was what he had come to; he was so lost, so confused, so devoid of all reason, that he had sought death —.

MY MOTHER'S MEMORY

Between 2006 and 2009 my mother and I would sit in her room at her nursing care facility and look at photographs. She was in her late nineties and normal conversation had become impossible. Slowly, carefully, I'd turn the old felt pages of one of our family photograph albums, hoping that old images of friends and family would remind her happily of the full life she'd once lived. Sometimes I'd sing to her the songs I loved as a boy—"Ricochet" or "The Tennessee Waltz"—and she'd try to sing along with me. Sometimes I'd sing the songs she used to sing to me when I was very young, like "She'll Be Coming 'Round the Mountain" and "Old Smokey," and she'd clap her hands and laugh at the silly, somewhat familiar verses. Or we'd look at photographs.

My mother's finger, which was becoming more and more like a claw, tapped a photograph.

"Amylu," I said. "You remember Amylu, my first girlfriend."

She paused a moment and said, "Oh yes. Bless her heart."

"She's about thirteen there. In junior high."

"She said she hoped you'd grow over the summer."

I laughed. This many years after Amylu's death, the jokey remark of a thirteen year-old girl was all that remained of her in my mother's memory. I'd heard the story a hundred times. A summer morning in 1956. I was away at camp in Vermont and my mother was weeding the front garden of our house in Great Neck. When Amylu and a girlfriend walked by, my mother waved and walked across the lawn to say hello. Amy told her that she'd just gotten a postcard from me. Then she said, "I sure hope he's grown over the summer."

Amy was tall for her age, while at fourteen I was just over five feet.

Some nights, when we were alone, away from prying eyes, I'd stand on a rock and kiss her goodnight.

"She was just joking, Mom."

"You weren't short, were you?"

"Sure, you remember. Dad told me not to worry because Phil Rizzuto was short and he was the Yankee shortstop. But then I grew five inches in one year. *And I guess that showed her!*"

This tickled my mother, as I knew it would, and she laughed the high, wonderful laugh I hadn't heard since I was a boy.

My mother touched another photograph of Amy, her high school graduation picture.

"She loved you."

"Well, she was a good friend."

"I think you played with her heart."

"She was my friend, Mom. I was in love with her in junior high school."

"She cried."

It was in August, 1962, a week before Amy began Freshman Orientation at RISD. I don't remember why she was having dinner with us. Probably my mother, who'd known Amy since she was twelve, wanted to mark the occasion. Amy was eighteen.

I have a vivid memory from that evening: Amy just stopped talking and tears streamed down her cheeks. She smiled lamely and shook her head, looking at her dinner plate, saying nothing. My mother said tenderly, "Oh honey, this must be a rough time for you. Going off to college is so stressful, leaving family and friends. But Amylu, you'll discover a whole new wonderful world," and she reached out and softly patted Amy's left hand.

That summer between my sophomore and junior year at college, I'd worked as a cue card boy on "Celebrity Talent Scouts," a CBS summer replacement television show. On Saturdays I'd pick

Amy up in Great Neck and we'd drive to Jones Beach. We'd play paddleball. We'd run into the ocean. I'd grab her and toss her into a wave. We were still like kids. Later, we'd rub suntan lotion on each other's back, lay on our towels, and talk. She hung on my words. I was older. I was her best friend. I told her about my boss, Irving Mansfield , who liked me, and his icy wife, Jacqueline Susann, who didn't. I told her about delivering scripts to Harry Belafonte and Robert Goulet and Carol Burnett. I told her about Jerry Lewis clowning around in rehearsal and cutting my tie with a scissor he kept in his pocket. I talked a lot about Faulkner because he'd just died. I'd just played Hamlet at college and would recite soliloquies to her. Sometimes I'd read Amy sections from Sharon's recent letters. Amy listened intently, but she didn't seem to find them as funny as I did.

I'd looked at Amy, my oldest friend, sitting across from me at the dining-room table, tears on her face, and I'd said nothing. Neither did my father. Emotional business was not his world. It was supposed to be my world, but, I too, had nothing to say. Amy had been my summer entertainment. It had all seemed so easy and light-hearted.

Without those old family photograph albums, my mother and I would have been at a loss for words. Until she died at ninety-nine, we'd sit side by side on the sofa in her small room, one of the four albums perched on both our knees. By then she'd become an almost permanently happy person, and the past that existed in these photographs, a past with which she had often found fault, was now funny and constantly surprising.

LETTERS

In the winter of 2003 I received a short letter from Robert Danzer informing me that his "dearest Helen" had passed away two weeks earlier, "a victim of melanoma cancer," and that he moved to California to be near Bob and his three grandchildren. I wasn't surprised—my parents' generation was dying.

Robert's script was tottery and the effort behind the writing touched me. I thought, I've become a friend of the family, someone who receives the courtesy of a handwritten note in a time of sorrow. It was, I recalled, the second note Robert had sent me.

I went into my bedroom and opened the drawer of an old desk where, over the years, I'd filed away bad news—obituaries, dear johns, funeral programs, denunciations, divorce decrees. And there, concealed behind a twenty–year-old postcard sent to me by an alcoholic friend who'd died in a car crash a week later, I found Robert's first note, written and mailed the day after the *Times* reported that the body of a young woman, Amylu Danzer, had washed ashore in Far Rockaway.

I remembered sitting on my unmade bed in Arizona Hall holding the unopened envelope in my hand. I'd just returned from Professor Rosenberg's lecture on Walter Pater and Pre-Raphaelite love poetry. It was April, a bright spring day in the city, a day full of Pater's "quickened sense of life," but, unlike Pater, I felt like I'd come to a standstill.

The envelope was addressed to "Mr John Rosenthal" in a grand and irritating script.

Of course, I thought, Mrs Danzer's an artist. Artists write like that.

I'd torn the envelope sideways, pulled out the card—a piece of fine, thin paper folded in half—and started to read. But it wasn't from Amy's mother. It was from Amy's father. Phrases had leaped out at me. "Wish to take this opportunity." "Thank you sincerely." "Your kind help."

A thank you note.

What had I expected?

An imperial signature stretched itself across the bottom of the second page. Robert C. Danzer. One word, every letter linked.

Now, forty years later, in the middle of middle-age, I sat down at the kitchen table, poured myself a cup of coffee, and placed both letters before me. As I pulled Robert's first letter from its old envelope—very gently this time—a yellowed two-inch newspaper clipping fell out and fluttered to the floor like a moth. A single paragraph noted that "Amy Lou Danzer" had been identified as the twenty-one year-old woman whose body had recently washed ashore at Beach 40th Street in Edgemere, Queens.

The notepaper was only four inches wide and Robert's script wasn't small. He was able to fit only three or four words on a line.

I read it again, and looked out of my kitchen window. At the bottom of my yard the waxy leaves of a spindly magnolia tree reflected a cold light. Across the street, a steep little hill of gray trees rose to a deck on which a small black dog paced. I thought, when I was twenty-two, the idea of John Keats dying in Rome, longing for Fanny Brawne, would bring me to tears, and yet in the presence of a living grief I'd responded only with irritation.

Mrs Danzer and I would like to take this opportunity to thank you sincerely for your kind help in the futile search for the young soul God had claimed weeks before.

I tried to remember the young man in 1965 sitting on his bed and reading that sentence. He was a literary type, who probably disapproved of the nebulous word "soul." But why, I wondered, did that same literary young man not appreciate the rich ambivalence contained in the next sentence? *I suppose we should be grateful that he finally revealed his dark secret to us all.* I'd read the note cursorily, feebly—I'd overlooked the grief that was barely contained beneath the language of a layered courtesy. *"Thank you, too, for all the happy hours you gave her."*

The two notes lay side by side on my kitchen table. Robert was now a very old man. His grand script had collapsed on itself.

That afternoon I found myself in the darkroom reworking one of my early city photographs. I don't remember which one it was, but I remember experiencing that peculiar kind of pensiveness that touches me whenever I spend time looking at my old images of places that have either been demolished or gentrified. Nothing unusual in that. An old photograph, with its sense of lost time, can turn into a melancholy object.

I thought, with Helen gone and Robert drifting away, Amy was about to enter the realm of oblivion—reduced to a few bleached photographs and a dusty painting on a basement shelf. I thought of Helen and I recalled her words: "I won't pretend there's a part of me that doesn't ache." Forty years is a long time to ache. A mother's memory. Different than ours. Over now.

BLOCKPRINT: HER WRITING

In 1992 a surprising piece of information came my way from Karen K., one of Amylu's RISD classmates. Amylu, it turned out, had published a few articles in the student magazine, *Blockprint.*

The information was timely because I was thinking of writing something about Amylu's suicide. Well, not her suicide exactly, but something beneath and around it, something obscure enough to have become the material of certain dreams that, in themselves, seemed to contain an appeal. In these dreams, Amy seemed to be saying, "You understand, don't you, that I'm not quite gone yet?"

Not quite gone yet. Such an appeal is as voiceless as a shadow, but it's heard by those who, for obscure reasons, incline towards the elegiac. I believed in the power of appeals, listened to them, sought them; my early life as a photographer depended on them. In 1972, as I walked around the Lower East Side with my first real camera, a man who had only recently taken on the responsibility of noticing things, I found myself photographing the signs of village life that still persisted on the margins of the city. Stacks of bread in the window of Jewish bakeries; retired Ukrainian men smoking and playing backgammon in Tompkins Square; a slice of sunlight filling the sails of a clipper ship in the window of an Italian Sailors Club on Mulberry Street. All around me I sensed a defenseless fragility, a future Manhattan in which all of these things would be absent.

I thought to myself, somebody's going to take all of this away. This won't last. It's slow, quiet, early twentieth-century stuff. These people haven't gotten the news. This is America after all. It'll be gone soon. Take the photograph. It's not much, but it's something. Wait, the light is too harsh. Come back later this afternoon when the sun starts to sink behind New Jersey. No, quick. Take it now.

Not quite gone yet.

The Manhattan real estate boom of the 1980s did the city in. People and places were gone overnight. Donald Trump and his friends moved in and built high-rises that cast shade all day over once sunny streets.

A few weeks later I drove from Chapel Hill to Providence and went straight to the archives of RISD's Fleet Library. (I felt a little breathless, as if I were going on a blind date.) *Blockprint*, I was told, had ceased publication in 1968 but all of the issues had been archived. I explained in general terms what I was looking for and the librarian vanished into the stacks. A few minutes later she returned carrying an armload of bound *Blockprints* published between the fall semester of 1962 and early February of 1965.

I found ten articles with the "Amylu Danzer" byline, written between March 1963 and February 1965.

The first nine of these articles were reviews of movies and campus events.

The tenth was not.

I wondered if I'd recognize her voice again, not the phantom voice floating in one of my dreams, but the real voice of my friend, her words, her own words—that voice whose absence, apparently (here I was in the Archives!) I never stopped missing. I wondered if I would encounter in Amy's prose (I'd never thought of her as a writer) the Amy that I'd known since she was twelve—only a little older and more thoughtful

More than anything, though, I wanted to know if the despair—mental illness?—that led to her suicide a year later had made an early appearance in her writing. Call it: a slight veering off course.

Reading her reviews in a bright, almost silent nook of the reading room, I realized immediately that I was being introduced to an Amylu I didn't know—an impatient, contentious, and dour Amylu. This Amylu's interests were varied—dance, poetry, painting, sociology, contemporary art, aesthetics—but as a critic she wasn't easily impressed. Ingmar Bergman's *The Seventh Seal* was "a far-fetched story … a medieval revival sermon." Elia Kazan's *America, America*—which had been nominated for Oscars as Best Picture, Best Screenplay and Best Director—was, according to Amylu, "indigestible." Even her compliments were backhanded. Attending a lecture by one of her professors on contemporary painting, Amylu approached something like approval, but didn't quite make it: "It cleared away more intellectual clutter than it created."

("Oh, Amylu was smart all right," Helen Danzer had said, as we sat on her screen porch. "Sometimes too smart for her own good." A sigh followed.)

Taciturnity, however, is not despondency—the gloom that envelops and perhaps kills the soul. And, in any case, crankiness can be kind of funny.

Of course any attempt to identify the mental state of a critic by reading between the lines of a review is next to impossible. In order to be known, to be disclosed, to be "caught," as it were, the critic must step outside the review—accidentally, perhaps parenthetically—to speak personally, anxiously, as if *it's necessary*. Fear, resentment, and even anger can often do the trick. And Amy finally obliged.

In the spring of her sophomore year Amylu attended a conference at Connecticut College which featured, among others, the revolutionary social critic, Paul Goodman. At one point, Goodman chided college professors for retreating into their expertise and failing to express opinions about the problems that plague America—racism, "infamous TV programming" etc. In a long parenthesis, Amy stepped outside the role of a critic and made a statement of her own:

(College becomes a retreat. The universities are growing; soon like in Medieval times when every third man was a monk, every third man may be a prof. Cinder block dormitories make good stoic buildings. By pushing the imagination we see the future terrain made up of university campuses, office buildings, and slum clearance projects.)

By any measure this was a grim response to Goodman's provocation and I wondered if sophomore art students in 1964 worried about a dreary, over-organized future America, barren of beauty? Perhaps Amylu had read Jane Jacobs' *The Death and Life of Great American Cities* with its dark depiction of urban renewal; perhaps she was familiar with Norman Mailer's diatribes against the "creeping totalitarianism" of American life. I wouldn't doubt it.

But nothing could have prepared me, then or now, for Amylu's response, a few paragraphs later, to Harold Taylor's almost lyrical description of the progressive education curriculum of Sarah Lawrence College. According to Taylor, a former president of Sarah Lawrence, knowledge wasn't achieved through suffering and grief—that was rubbish, old-school, Artaud's artist signaling through the flames. The new model of learning required gentle and personal guidance—students (painters, sculptors, composers) working on individual projects with thoughtful assistance from their professors.

I would have expected Amylu to find this progressive model of education congenial, with its focus on the individual, not the classroom, with its sensitivity to the idiosyncratic personality that might not "blend in." But not only did she not admire this new pedagogical model, she found it disabling and degrading. This time she dropped the parenthesis and spoke directly to the reader, with fervor:

Pushing this idea to its extreme the educational institution becomes a rehabilitation center for the mentally unhealthy products of contemporary culture. And why is this an extreme? Where else would the thousands go who have spent fifteen years in classrooms getting lessons in the occupation

137

of studentry? High school entrance requirements and in-flated tuitions select those adults that will best concede to four more years of care and feeding with trained babysitters, or in the more progressive schools, hospitalization.

In the light of her subsequent suicide, now less than a year away, it's difficult not to read into this paragraph an ominous suggestion that Amylu was beginning to regard RISD, with its "inflated tuitions," as just another "rehabilitation center for the mentally unhealthy products of contemporary culture."

Yet I don't think so. I think this paragraph is an angry (almost Swiftian) denunciation of Taylor's assertion that the journey to self-knowledge isn't steep and arduous, but rather, level and smooth and sanitary and safe. Re-reading Lucy W.'s letter describing her own "traumatic" training at RISD—the unsparing demand that one must look "deeply within the self"—I can easily imagine that Amy, under the influence of her formidable professors, had little sympa-thy for Taylor's progressive schooling of young artists at Sarah Law-rence—rich girls coddled into bogus self-realization.

I left the Fleet Library with photocopies of Amylu's *Blockprint* articles, and, over the years, I've re-read them. They've been in my possession for over two decades—long enough to have yielded up whatever secrets they contained. And no, I didn't find a lost and de-spondent Amylu. I found a young woman, a good writer, who was smart but lacked (or repressed?) a sense-of-humor, who didn't care what her peers thought, and who seemed to foresee, in the not-so-distant future, a large American failure—ugly diminished cities in which university students were nursed through the illness of being alive. This darkness is indeed unusual in a nineteen year-old, and I've wondered if her dark view turned truly dystopic and eventually undermined the worth of the world she was obliged to inhabit. But I have no way of knowing that. Still, I keep it in mind. It's important to remember that mental illness and mental darkness are not always the same thing.

"The world is crazy, not me," Amylu shouted as she stormed up the beach.

Years later, for no discernible reason, I remembered the question I'd asked Amy in the spring of 1962 when she told me gleefully that she'd been accepted at the Rhode Island School of Design. "But how will you get a good education?" I'd said with the assurance of a man who had turned foolishness into a way of life. "Can you take courses in the modern novel? Shakespeare?"

LIONEL TRILLING IN FOREST HILLS

Early September, 1964, New York City.

S omewhere between sleeping and waking, I wondered where I was. The usual sounds of summer were missing—the rattle of the cracked air-conditioner above my head, the crowing rooster across Route 158. Nothing. Sweet silence. I rolled over, blinked, and looked sideways at the room. Daylight shimmering behind Venetian blinds. Not too early. Beside my bed, a bulky, reddish, creature-like object. The honeyed smell of pipe tobacco. Only my father watched television on a Barcalounger, only my father smoked a pipe. I was in the den of my parents' apartment in Manhattan, lying on a sofa bed.

Five stories below me, horns were honking.

Home. Mind my manners.

I was twenty-one.

Two nights earlier, in Winston-Salem, North Carolina, after the final curtain call for *Pajama Game*, we'd gathered on the Tanglewood Barn stage, actors and techies, and we'd drunk a few beers and said our dramatic goodbyes. Quarrels were brushed away like fluff. True and false compliments were paid. Summer love affairs ended quietly, with or without promises. A successful summer-stock season. Packed houses every night. The next morning, yesterday, I'd tossed everything—books, clothes, typewriter—in the back of my Volkswagen and driven straight to the city. My life in North Carolina, which began as a freshman at Wake Forest College in 1960, was over.

I opened the blinds and looked out at 57th Street, still shadowed. A few of the higher windows were beginning to pick up sunlight.

I thought of Ned. Every morning, rain or shine, I'd watch Ned paddle around the stagnant pond in the middle of Turner's Trailer Court. Ned was a patient duck, who waited every morning for me to show up with Cheerios. Quacking, he'd almost fly across the algae when he'd see me approach his pond, yellow box in hand. Sometimes, when I'd return to my trailer after a performance, I'd see Ned in my headlights, feathers fluffed, sleeping on the muddy edge of the still pond.

I thought of Sharon, back home now in Ohio after her summer waitressing in Winston-Salem. I pictured her in the tiny bedroom of my trailer, slipping out of her sky-blue waitress uniform, unpinning her waitress bonnet, a sly half-smile on her face. I'd take that smile into the future. It would be my secret. It was always my secret.

We'd decided to get married next summer, after her senior year at Wake.

I sighed.

In a week I'd be moving uptown to Arizona Hall on 114th Street to begin my life as an English doctoral student at Columbia. "You must be thrilled!" everybody said. "A PhD from Columbia!" But, no, I wasn't thrilled. Playing Hamlet was thrilling. Playing Henry Higgins. The curtain slowly opening, the bright hot band of scuffed radiant stage, the shining first row faces, the soft murmur as disbelief is suspended, a busy street in Covent Garden, a dark castle in Denmark—that was thrilling.

From the apartment window, I watched a dozen taxis weaving in and out of lanes and I recalled conversations I'd had over the years with New York actors, glad for the summer work in North Carolina. "My life. I audition and eat and drive a cab. That's my life." "My boyfriend did *A Doll House* at Theater Four last year and he's been driving a taxi ever since."

Is that what I was afraid of? Had I chickened out on life?

I thought, I'm bored. I'll call Amylu. My first girlfriend in junior high and now my oldest friend. We'll hang out. We always hang out. If it's warm enough, I'll pick her up and we'll drive to Jones Beach and I'll tell her about Tanglewood and the roles I played. I'll tell her about John Hillerman, the New York actor who played my uncle in *The Little Foxes* and told me I could be the next Montgomery Clift. I'll tell her about the fight Sharon and I had three weeks ago. I'd been talking to Amylu since she was thirteen, reading her poems, chapters from books, doing my impersonations. Kirk Douglas. Marlon Brando. I was older than her, and two grades ahead.

I lay back in bed and read a few pages of Philip Roth's *Letting Go*. I put it down and wrote a letter to Sharon. "I'm already bored. My parents have new furniture. A man from Bloomingdale's gave their apartment a new look. Blond. Roth's book is pretty good. It's not like *Goodbye, Columbus*. You wouldn't like it. Sex and desperation among English teachers. Or maybe you would. Where are you? In your room? What are you wearing? Never mind. Send me your panties. The black ones with the lacy edges. And the red ones. I have an altar in mind at Columbia."

I dressed and wandered barefoot into the living-room. It was beige and spotless. Down the thick carpeted hallway I could faintly hear my mother singing as she put on her make-up.

Only two days since *Pajama Game* closed, but I missed Tanglewood—the sweaty performances, the flubbed lines and ad libs, the stained costumes and theater gossip. What a famous actor said backstage. Brando this, Brando that.

I didn't miss my trailer or the strip of buzzing flypaper hanging over the fold-out Formica table in my kitchen.

I called Amy again. No answer. I also wanted to tell her about a Dylan song I'd just heard.

In the postscript of a letter Amy had sent me over the summer, she'd written that she'd be home from her job in Rhode Island by early September and we should get together then. She couldn't wait to see me. She'd call me.

So where was she? I phoned her again. No answer.

I sat on the beige sofa and thumbed through a magazine, opened and closed a silver cigarette case with my father's initials embossed on its lid—two rows of perfectly stacked Winstons on red velvet. Nice.

Nobody lived like their parents anymore.

I crossed the room, opened my mother's music box, pulled its crank gently. Beautiful with its deep, rosewood luster. In junior high school, Amy would come over and want to play it. She'd watch wide-eyed as the brass cylinder began to turn, its teeth plucking the pins as it played "Daughter of the Regiment." "When I was old enough to perform chores," my mother told us, "I'd play the music box and dance around the parlor, dusting. Isn't that silly?" And she'd laugh sweetly, as if she were seven.

Music box, parlor, Tennessee—my mother was a little exotic to Amy, whose parents were born in Brooklyn.

Then the phone rang.

I still remember her voice coming through the line. "It's Amy-lu," she said. Not "Hi Johnny!"

"Amy!" I said, suddenly not bored. "I've been calling you!"

"I'm not at home."

"Where are you?"

"At my grandmother's."

"Your grandmother's?" I'd forgotten she had a grandmother. Of course she had a grandmother.

"Where does she live?"

"Forest Hills."

"Oh. How was your summer? Do you miss your children?"

We should have been laughing by now, the telephone charged with affection.

"Children?"

"The artist's kids in Providence," I said lightly. "You wrote me about them. Do you miss them?" I was making small talk, which I never made with Amy.

"Oh." She paused. "I guess."

In July Amy had written me a letter that my mother had forwarded to Tanglewood. We rarely wrote each other. The handwriting on the page was large and almost childish, her sentences sloping; the return address consisted of a single word "Amylu." She wrote that she was in Warwick, Rhode Island for the summer, taking care of two young children while their father, one of her professors at the RISD, traveled around Italy on a grant. She described beach days with plastic buckets and shovels, sand-castles, and rainy days with art projects on a sun porch, beads, and finger-painting. She wrote that she took long walks and heard voices above her head, beautiful voices, and that every morning she'd find bright pennies in the mailbox. I'd wondered what she meant. Did she have a secret admirer? "Oh, Amy," I said to myself, as if Amylu was given to whimsy, which she wasn't. But I was late for rehearsal and didn't think much about it.

"Any more magical pennies?"

Amy was silent. Had she forgotten what she'd said in her letter?

"When do you go back to RISD?" I asked.

"I don't know. In a few days."

"Okay, let's hang out. Columbia doesn't start for another week."

"I'm at my Grandmother's."

"I know. When are you going back to Great Neck?"

"I don't know."

I wondered if Amy was ill or half-asleep, if her grandmother was an old person who disliked excitement. I wondered why she was speaking in a monotone and what she was doing at her grandmother's.

I began to tell her about my summer. I told her that I'd played the lead in *Time Remembered*, the Anouilh play, the same role Richard Burton played on Broadway. I told her about John Hillerman, who talked with a British accent and who was inseparable from his whippet, Lizzie, a thin, delicate dog who ran blind when she was let off her leash. I told her that when the season ended he gave me a gift: a record of Otto Klemperer conducting Brahms's *Second Symphony*.

I heard breathing on the other end of the line.

I described my trailer and Turner's Trailer Court. It was an inferno, I told her. Bugs the size of shoes. Barking dogs tied to ropes. One tiny air-conditioner that barely worked. Rednecks yelling at their wives. "Behind my trailer was a scummy pond that contained one duck. I fed him Cheerios."

From Amy: breathing.

I imitated the drawl of the guys who worked at the Purina silo across the street when they talked about their dogs. That kind of thing always cracked her up.

More breathing.

"You ever hear Brahms's *Second Symphony?*"

"I don't know."

"Ever see a dog run blind?"

"What does that mean?"

I was in mid-air.

"Amy."

"What?"

"What's wrong?"

"Nothing."

"You called me and you're not talking."

Again, silence.

Suddenly I was annoyed. Who was I talking to?

"Okay, then," I said cheerfully, "I'll give you a call at Thanksgiving. We'll get together then."

A fierce, angry voice came across the line, a voice on the edge of tears. *"It's not so far that you can't come see me!"*

In all the years I'd known Amylu I'd never heard this voice. The pencil I'd been nervously tapping against a pad of paper almost jumped out of my hand.

"Okay, okay, Amy." I said. "Just give me directions. I know where Forest Hills is, but that's about it."

Amy put her grandmother on the phone, a brisk old woman who cleared her throat and led me through the Mid-Town Tunnel to the 108th Street exit and then through a variety of left and right turns to a semi-detached house with green canvas awnings on Kessel Street. Finished, she asked me sternly if I'd like to speak to Amylu. Sure, I said, thank you. Then I told Amy, happily, in our usual manner, that I'd see her in about an hour, and she said, All right.

Half an hour later, as I drove through the grim florescence of the Mid-Town tunnel, it dawned on me that Amy's behavior on the phone was that of someone whose heart had been broken. Those beautiful voices in the sky, the magical pennies she'd found in her mailbox. Had that been Amy's lyrical way of describing the experience of falling in love? If so, then her numbing silences this morning suggested she'd been crushed and was grief-stricken. Had Amylu ever experienced heartbreak? I didn't think so.

By the time I'd turned off the L.I.E. onto 108th Street, I knew that Amylu needed me, her oldest friend, to help her through this; in fact she'd demanded it. "It's not so far that you can't come see me!"

But I had to be careful. I had to play my role well; not over-do it. I remembered a director telling me during a rehearsal to quit acting. I said, "I don't understand. You don't want me to *act*? Isn't that what I'm supposed to do? "Yes, quit acting," he said. "You seem to know what you're going to say before you say it." He told me to look at the other actors, and listen to what they're saying and react to the words coming out of their mouths. Be in the moment.

I thought, listen to Amylu, look her in the eye and listen to her. Don't act.

I pressed the bell, propping the screen door open with my left hand. A faint chime floated out of the house. Looking back now, I observe myself—tenderly, I admit—standing there as if I were a leading man about to make an entrance. A few butterflies, of course. Amy was heartbroken, she was hurting, but I'd set it right; it was a role I could play with my eyes closed. I'd always made her happy, ever since we were kids diving for pennies at the Lake Success community pool. Friendship couldn't replace love, but it could come close.

I'd write Sharon tonight and tell her how I'd helped Amylu through a bad time.

Across the street a fat Dalmatian lay on the top step of a porch, blinking sleepily, its chin resting on its forepaws. A breeze rustled the old oaks lining the street. I rang the bell again. Silence. Rapped softly on the door. Someone coming down stairs. The clicking of multiple locks and the door swung inward—slowly, guardedly. I arranged a smile on my face. Hurry up, Grandma.

But it wasn't Amylu's grandmother standing in the doorway eyeing me suspiciously. It was Amy—Amy in light blue Bermuda shorts and a wrinkled, white blouse, Amy with a dull, bloated face, a glistening forehead, and a livid patch of cheek impressed with the recognizable pattern of corduroy. Behind her, in a dark room, thin bars of light from a shuttered window fell on old brocaded furniture.

I thought, She looks ill, and started to say something jokey, but Amy cut me off. "I know you hate people who take naps, but I don't care." Then she said, "Wait," and turned into the house.

I stepped back and let the screen door close.

What had just happened? Hate people who take naps? I'd said that when I was fourteen. I remembered saying it. I also hated people who drank coffee.

I could hear her speaking softly to someone inside the house, possibly in disagreement. Then the door opened and she joined me on the front stoop, chewing on a thumbnail, eyes squinting and looking downward. We stood there awkwardly until I suggested a walk and she mumbled "Okay," still nibbling at her thumb.

A few things I recall about the neighborhood, not much: the glimmering disc of a grandfather clock behind a screen door; a tilted mailbox with a blue heron painted on its side; small driveways separating the parlor of one house from the bedroom of the next.

Walking beside me Amy seemed drugged, not heartbroken.

And I, the leading man, was ad-libbing.

("Pipe down," I want to say to him, after all this time.)

147

Our conversation comes back to me in fragments.

"You know e.e. cummings? 'Nobody, not even the rain, has such small hands.' Listen: 'The Cambridge ladies who live in furnished souls /Are unbeautiful and have comfortable minds.' I love that. I also love the way he describes the moon rattling 'like a fragment of angry candy.'"

I looked at Amy. She wasn't even smiling.

We walked through a neighborhood full of large, half-timbered houses with pointed gables; acorns, still wearing their crowns, were scattered on grass and pavement; sprinklers tossed out bright lassos of water. And I went on.

Had she heard Dylan's last album?

No, apparently.

Last summer we'd sung "Don't Think Twice" on our way to Jones Beach.

"There's a great lyric. He's talking about the past and he says, 'Ah, but I was so much older then, I'm younger then than ...' Wait, wait, I screwed it up." I tried it again, articulating the words slowly. 'Ah ... but I was so much older then ... I'm younger than that now.' Dylan." I said, shaking my head.

I wanted to repeat it, but I received no encouragement.

"Ever hear of Lionel Trilling?"

"No."

"Ever read Wordsworth's 'Immortality Ode'?"

"I don't know."

"You don't know?"

I wanted to talk about Lionel Trilling. At the moment nothing seemed more important to me than talking about Lionel Trilling.

"Trilling wrote an essay about Wordsworth's 'Ode.' He argued that Wordsworth wasn't bidding farewell to his poetic powers when he wrote 'Though nothing can bring back the hour/ Of splendor in the grass / Of glory in the flower.' You remember *Splendor in the Grass*, with Warren Beatty and Natalie Wood?"

"Yes."

"I applied to Columbia because Lionel Trilling teaches there."

I waited.

The words "Lionel Trilling" hung inanely in the air.

Amy mumbled something.

"What?"

"I visited Bob in Illinois."

"Who?"

"My brother."

"Oh. Illinois?"

"He worked at a John Deere plant all summer."

"What's that?"

"They make tractors."

"Boring."

"No, the machines were beautiful, not boring."

I thought: RISD talk.

I told Amy she needed to read Walker Percy's *The Moviegoer*.

I also remember this: Amy murmuring something about a book she'd read, still nibbling at her thumb, eyes unfocused. She didn't remember the title. Erich Fromm.

"He's a psychologist," she said.

"Any good?"

She started to answer but I cut her off saying that the best psychologists were novelists—Melville, Faulkner, Henry James—and that if she wanted real psychology she should read *Moby Dick*, not Erich Fromm. I told her I wouldn't go to a shrink if my life depended on it. "Name one great artist who's normal."

Amy said, "He's not that kind of psychologist."

On our way back to Kessel Street, I told her about my recent quarrel with Sharon. I wanted to stop talking but I didn't know how. I was like an actor onstage with someone who'd forgotten their lines.

A white-haired, reddish old man was washing a black convertible in his driveway, listening to a ballgame on a transistor radio. "Three two, Yankees," he said, happily—an Irishman with a sponge in his hand, a normal person. I smiled and nodded in acknowledgment.

I told Amylu that this summer Sharon was working the lunch shift at a steak house in Winston and everyday a golfing pal of the manager's came in and sat in one of her booths. A tall guy about thirty who owned a chain of grocery stores. "Can you imagine having a golfing pal?" I asked Amy.

No response.

I described how he began to hang out after lunch, talking about the good old days when he was a basketball star at a small college in South Carolina. Then he started bringing her little gifts—one day a basket of peaches, then a watermelon. "Sharon said he was just a big, friendly Southern guy and there was nothing to get upset about, but I knew what he wanted. He offered her a private tour of his beer cooler." I laughed, but Amy didn't. "Anyway, one night I made her call him up while I listened in on the other line. I made her tell him she had a boyfriend and she was in love with him and he shouldn't bring her any more gifts. It was a difficult—"

"You did what?" Amy asked quietly.

"I made her call the guy—"

"You *made* her?"

"I didn't make her. I told her—"

"You listened in?"

"Yes."

"Why?"

"What do you mean, why? So I could hear what she said to him!"

"Did Sharon know you were listening?"

"Yes."

"And she let you?"

"Yes."

Why did she do that?"

"I would have broken up with her if she didn't."

Amy looked at me, her lips slightly twisted. Specks of spittle clung to the corner of her mouth.

She said something inaudible and turned away.

"What?"

"You've become a businessman," she whispered.

150

It was a code word between us, with wings powerful enough to carry me back to the beginnings of our friendship, when we'd talk about what mattered to us, and what didn't. I'd told her I hated golf and mood music. She told me she'd never wear make-up. We both loved poetry—Kahlil Gibran, Walter de la Mare. We didn't care about possessions. The people who mattered the most were artists. The people who mattered the least were businessmen.

Enraged, I swallowed once with difficulty, thinking, *Sharon and I are lovers, lovers fight and hurt each other, lovers fuck, we fuck on floors, against walls, at drive-ins ... What do you know about sex? ... You've never even been in love, you don't know what being in love is ... Sharon thought she was pregnant, we would have been kicked out of school ... I read her poems, I read her "The Love Song of J. Alfred Prufrock," all of it ... I explained Lionel Trilling to her ... Sometimes we have the same thoughts at the same time, that's what love is ...* But all I said was, "Sharon apologized, and everything's okay now. We're going to get married next summer." If I'd expected a reaction to this bit of news, I didn't get one: Amylu no longer seemed interested in the conversation.

A few minutes later, as we approached her grandmother's house, I felt only confusion. As if I were in a dream, nothing was as it should be. Who was this stranger walking beside me? Where had Amylu gone? Her light-heartedness, easy laughter? Ever since we were kids I'd see in her eyes an admiration for the special person I hoped I was. Friends look at each other that way. But this person didn't even look at me. She looked down. Did she know who I was? Did she care? Who was she?

I thought, I've got to get out of here.

I told her I needed to beat the traffic and Amy mumbled something and turned away.

As I drove around Forest Hills looking for the 108th Street access to the Long Island Expressway, I thought: Tractors. Beautiful?

I thought, I'm not a boring person.

What did she mean, "It's not so far away you can't come see me"?

On the drive back to the city, I re-played my visit with Amylu, I repeated phrases, parsed inflections and measured the extent of my miscalculations. I'd imagined myself to be an actor, assured, handsome, splendid on the doorstep, and wreathed in soft suburban light. I'd arrived to spring Amy from the company of a boring old woman. To help her endure the heartache of love. My audience would be familiar, appreciative. Yet I'd flopped. And my audience turned out to be asleep. It was crazy and confusing. I pictured Amylu bursting out of the waves at Jones Beach, water streaming down her face, her long glossy legs staggering in the thick sand, her laughter. Thirteen. Sixteen. Then nineteen.

Years later, in the spirit of friendly self-mockery, I observe my younger self driving back to the city on that fall afternoon. My feelings were wounded because my oldest friend had just treated me coldly, unpleasantly, and strangely. I find it odd (but still touching) that it never once occurred to me that Amy might have continued to act just as coldly and unpleasantly and strangely after she'd returned to her grandmother's house.

I was twenty-one. I found it hard to worry about other people.

At home, I found my mother in the kitchen chopping carrots and potatoes for a pot roast. Sinatra's *Songs for Swingin' Lovers* was playing in the living room. It was her favorite album during those years. She asked me how Amylu was doing. She probably thought I was going to say, "She's fine. She sends her best," but instead I said, "I don't know. She didn't seem like herself."

My mother didn't say anything, not for a while anyway, and I wondered if she was concentrating on her recipe. Certainly, her reply, when it finally arrived, wasn't what I expected. "Well, if you ask me," she said, as she began to peel an onion, dabbing her eyes with her wrist, "I always thought Amylu was a little odd."

I knew we were at the edge of a conversation that would turn sour. That happened a lot in those years. We didn't know each other anymore. For a moment I wanted to defend Amy—all my friends, really—against my mother's condescension; I wanted to

152

say to my mother, in the angry voice of those years, "It's only odd people who matter!" but that was the kind of thing I'd say to my friends, not to my mother.

In less than a week I would find myself among people who, unlike Amylu or my mother, appreciated Lionel Trilling. By then I would have launched myself into a life I didn't want, a nervous life that included only fleeting thoughts of Amylu. When I heard in February that she'd been asked to leave RISD and that, three days later, she'd disappeared at Jones Beach, I felt something like embarrassment. Had I missed something? Had Amy demanded my presence in Forest Hills so I could see that something was happening to her? Had I missed that? A few days after I'd seen Amy in Forest Hills, I simply regarded our visit as an irritating anomaly, fully expecting that the next time we got together—Thanksgiving? Christmas?—she would have lightened up and returned to the Amylu I had always known. But I never saw her again. In the middle of April her body, or what was left of it, floated onto a beach in East Rockaway.

But on that September day, as Sinatra sang "Anything Goes," I left my mother in the kitchen and went into my room. I wanted to get back to *Letting Go*. Paul and Libby's marriage was falling apart. Everybody was yelling and sobbing and snarling and accusing, everybody was confused. Roth never let up. I'd look up from the book, my teeth clenched in something like bewilderment. It was almost wonderful not to be these people, to float above their predicaments on a bright river of prose. I also wanted to write Sharon a letter. I wanted to tell her that she was the only person in the world who really understood me, that I loved her and missed her, and that, as we both knew, we were meant for each other.

We broke up in April, a week before we ordered the invitations to our wedding in July.

* * *

One day, thirty years later, the thought crossed my mind that

153

I'd like to see a professional hypnotherapist. It was a semi-idle thought, prompted by a remark I'd overheard in a bar. Yes, the speaker assured his date, hypnosis can take you back in time. I was leaving the bar when I'd heard this odd remark, but it stuck with me. Would it be possible, I wondered, to return, in a hypnotic state, to that September day—to those quiet Forest Hill streets, to Amylu herself? I'd missed a great deal that day; I wasn't looking for anything in particular, so I didn't see anything in particular. Yet what if I were given the chance to see now what I couldn't see then? Perhaps, I thought, I could I find a hypnotherapist, who, like a poet, would lead me to that half-opened front door and that unhappy young woman who frowned at me as if I were a stranger?

I decided against it. I was too skeptical. It wouldn't work for me. And, in any case, such a return might not be a blessing. The dream of fleshing out the immateriality of memory, of recapturing some bright moment in the past before it had become dim and irrelevant, must be very ancient—fathoms deeper than nostalgia— but what, I wondered, is the point? I'd return to Forest Hills armed with words like "depression" and "bipolar disorder," and although I'd know that the lost can sometimes be found, what use would this knowledge be? Lacking the power to advise, or more specifically, to protect, I could only observe that lovely fall day through the lens of anguish.

WILLIAM EBERT

Phone conversation, October 9, 2016

"I know this is an odd question to ask, but are you the William Ebert who, more than fifty years ago, discovered the body of a young woman on a beach at Far Rockaway? The local newspaper said that a man named William Ebert was fishing and spotted the body and called the police."

"Yeah, that's me. They put my name in the newspaper, but, you know, they don't always tell the truth. We weren't fishing. Nothing like that. We were strolling along the boardwalk heading to work and we saw something on the sand that looked like a body."

"I'm so glad I tracked you down. I went online and typed in the name William Ebert and found an Ebert living in Valley Stream, Long Island who'd once lived Far Rockaway. And it's you! Amazing. Well, I'm writing a memoir about the woman whose body floated up that day. Can I ask you a few questions? Just a few."

"Sure."

"The paper said you were with a man named George Roberts."

"Georgie, he was a good friend of mine. We were on our way to work and we looked at the beach and saw the body. Georgie passed away a long time ago."

"How old were you then?"

"Let's see. It was 1965, right? I must have been 26."

"What was your job in Far Rockaway?"

"I was in plumbing then. We were working on the beach bungalows at 59th Street. They had a hundred bungalows up there. We

155

walked to work on the boardwalk every morning."

"So you weren't strolling, you were walking to work."

"We were strolling." (laughter)

"That must have been a shock."

"Sure it was. We didn't know what it was at first. But it turned out to be a body. There was no hair. And bloated you know. We didn't know if it was a man or a woman. There'd been a plane crash recently so we thought it was one of the bodies from that. Actually, now that I think of it, there were three of us there, not two like the paper said. A guy named Jimmy. We'd given him work for a couple of days. He's passed away too. He turned the body over with his foot and then yelled out, 'It's a woman.' She was wearing a bra and dungarees, that's all. The paper said she'd slipped off a rock and fell into the water. I think they said she was a blue-eyed blond and beautiful, an art student somewhere, but they say a lot of things."

"Well, she was blond and blue-eyed and beautiful, but that stuff about slipping off a rock wasn't true. She'd disappeared at Jones Beach two months before you saw her. The *Times* said a patrolman had seen her enter the water and hit her head on the rocks, but nobody saw anything, and there's no rocks or jetties on Jones Beach. Just sand and dunes. They made that up, maybe out of consideration for Amy's parents. I hope so. So what happened then?"

"We called the police."

"From a phone booth?"

"Yeah, in those days there were lots of phone booths on the boardwalk. Not anymore."

"What were your thoughts about finding the body?"

"Bad."

"Did it stay with you a long time?"

"No, not really. I'd say about a week. You can't think about something like that for a long time. You know, it's funny. I never pick up the phone, but I saw the name Rosenthal on my answering machine and I picked it up. I worked as a building superintendent for thirty years for a guy named Rosenthal, so I picked it up thinking it might have been someone from his family. He died a long time ago."

ALL DAY AND ALL NIGHT

from Amylu Danzer's Last Essay,
published two weeks before her death, February 10, 1965

All day and all night cars roll up Waterman Street and run down Angell Street. Between these two roads, sunk into or resting on some split level of the dormitory complex, Homer Hall rides the hill to overlook Providence.

Is it there to provide sufficient walled space for each female student?

How few inches, breadth and height can be lived—cramped?

The ceilings are low and treated efficiently—they stifle the sounds, leave only the noise: the phone, the buzzer, and the cars plowing up and down these two roads. The dorm provides for each girl a standard bed, table, desk, and self-standing mirror—small enough for a face. Short and narrow, scissored by efficiency, made of pale and sanded pine, the furniture is sub-pleasant. The closet and drawers sit complacently together behind sliding doors. To move these doors, a metal depression, almost deep enough for fingertips. Would a more human design demand a handle?

Because space is scarce, they do provide—though overheated and without windows—a workroom ... more practical to find a window than to ask no-one for air.

157

The refectory provides sufficient food—conveniently cooked? Given meat and vegetables cooked and over-cooked, the student often eats the appearance of food. Each night the student chooses to wait out the line or wait until 6:15, when so shortly after—confronted by a large boy demanding trays—you must rush a meal hardly begun. He has no time. You have no time. Who is giving out the time?

Amylu's wish for more congenial accommodation is entirely understandable, and so is her description of the deadening effects of bland functionality. Frankly, she sounds like any other sane and angry student of that era who dreaded a future in which undifferentiated people would live inside undifferentiated structures. Her complaints are specific and clear-headed and well-written. Her thinking is not disorganized. She's describing life in a prison. Inedible food she is rushed to eat. Everybody in a hurry. She's in a hurry. "Who is giving out the time?" she asks.

On the same day this article was published in *Blockprint* Amylu folded up a charcoal drawing of my Volkswagen barreling down the dunes at Jones Beach, stuck it in a small envelope, and mailed it to me: Johnny Rosenthal, Columbia University. With that insufficient address, it took ten days to reach me.

ALL DAY AND ALL NIGHT

All day and all night cars roll up Waterman Street and run down Angell Street. Between these two roads, sunk into or resting on some split level of the dormitory complex, Homer Hall rides the hill to overlook Providence. Is it there to provide sufficient walled space for each female student? How few inches, breadth and height can be lived—cramped?

The ceilings are low and treated efficiently — they stifle the sounds, leave only the noise: the phone, the buzzer, and the cars plowing up and down these two roads. The dorm provides for each girl a standard bed, table, desk, and self-standing mirror—small enough for a face. Short and narrow, scissored by efficiency, made of pale and sanded pine, the furniture is sub-pleasant. The closet and drawers sit compactly together behind sliding doors. To move those doors, a metal depression, almost deep enough for fingertips. Would a more human design demand a handle?

Because space is scarce, they do provide—though overheated and without windows — a workroom . . . more practical to find a window than to ask no-one for some air.

The refectory provides sufficient

(CONTINUED ON PAGE 8)

ALL DAY — NIGHT
(CONTINUED FROM PAGE 4)

food — conveniently cooked? Each night the student chooses to wait out the line or wait until 6:15, when so shortly after—confronted by a large boy demanding trays — the student must rush a meal hardly begun. He has no time. You have no time. Who is giving out the time?

AMYLU DANZER

LOLITA: THE SKETCH

I look for it in the college texts that sit unopened on the top shelf of the bookcase in my bedroom. Books like John Gassner's *Treasury of the Theater: Ibsen to Ionesco* and *English Prose of the Victorian Era*. The sketch I'm looking for was folded at least twice, so I look for a gap between the pages. If the book is in good condition, I turn it upside down and gently run my thumb across the pages. I perform this same ritual every three or four years. I look only in the books I owned before 1972 because that's when the sketch disappeared—after my first wife and I returned from our long sojourn on Crete and moved into a small cinderblock house in Carrboro, North Carolina.

We'd just had a baby and I'd decided to become a photographer.

On February 20, 1965, a cold, bright Saturday morning, I'd returned to Arizona Hall after eating a late breakfast at the coffee shop on the corner of Amsterdam and 113th Street. The mail was usually delivered around 11, and I was hoping to receive a letter from Sharon. Her last two letters had been disappointing, full of news about her roommate whose boyfriend, a Kappa Alpha, was breaking up with her. I didn't care about her roommate, or her boyfriend; all I cared about was how much Sharon loved me. Instead of a letter from Sharon, however, I pulled out a thick envelope addressed—in jittery, childishly printed capital letters—to Johnny Rosenthal, Columbia University, New York City. No return address. Someone with little neat handwriting—who?—had filled in my Arizona Hall street address, and, against all odds, the thick envelope, with its single comically insufficient five cent stamp, had been delivered. Holding it in my hands (it looked as if it had been rained on) I thought: a child who doesn't know how the postal system works has mailed me something—but I don't know any children. The postmark read Providence, RI, 2PM, February 10, 1965.

Ten days ago?

RI?

Rhode Island.

Rhode Island School of Design.

Amylu.

We hadn't seen each other since September. It had been a terrible visit. She barely talked and kept nibbling on her thumb.

I tore open the envelope and extracted an 18" × 24" sheet of drawing paper folded twice. A charcoal drawing—a violent tangle of lines. I turned it this way and that until a recognizable shape appeared: the humped hood of a Volkswagen.

The rest was easy: a dune, an ocean, tire tracks.

Jones Beach. The quick breeze blowing paper napkins across the sand. Waves thundering. Children shrieking. Laughter. Reading out loud. We spread Coppertone on each other's back.

I was touched. The drawing was a mid-winter gift from Amylu, an affectionate reference to one of our shared jokes, a piece of nonsense nobody else would care about. Two years earlier, as we were driving to Jones Beach, Amy had informed me that Lolita, my car (named after Kubrick's film) could float. According to her brother, Volkswagens were air-tight. Amy then proposed that we take Lolita for a dip in the ocean. "And we can share our lunch with her. There's more than enough." But in the parking lot at Jones Beach I said, "Sorry, Lolita, maybe next time," and I dabbed Coppertone on her insignia. This silly joke was repeated all summer long.

Now, in the drawing, Lolita was finally getting her chance. She was barreling down a dune, waves in the foreground.

Was Amy apologizing for the way she'd acted in September?

161

Even to be reminded of such distant, summertime whimsy—standing beside the fire extinguisher in the dark lobby of Arizona Hall—lightened my spirit. I was unhappy at Columbia, weighed down by a clammy seriousness

I thought, Thank you, Amy. I accept your apology. And I made a mental note to call Mrs Danzer later that day. She'd give me Amy's telephone number, and then Amy and I would talk and I'd tell her about my classmate from Yale who served me tea and declared that Faulkner was a bore. We'd pretend that our visit in September never occurred.

However, once I was in my room I decided to put off calling Mrs Danzer until later in the week.

I tossed Amy's drawing on my desk where, a day or two later, it was buried under a couple of Ann Radcliffe novels that I was reading for my master's thesis on *The Borderers*.

That was on Saturday.

Four days later, on the following Thursday, my mother called and told me that she'd just received a distressed phone call from Amylu's mother. Amy had been asked to leave RISD for medical reasons, and, three days later, had disappeared at Jones Beach.

After we hung up I remember standing in my room, immobile, barely breathing.

Later that afternoon I remembered Amy's charcoal sketch.

I fished the torn envelope out of my wastebasket and stared at the childlike letters, the almost useless address. I found the drawing, now smudged, under the Radcliffe books. I opened my window, and, slanting the paper downward, blew a tiny cloud of charcoal powder over 114th Street.

Maybe, I thought, the drawing wasn't an apology.

Later in the afternoon, Mrs Danzer called me and filled in a few details concerning Amy's disappearance at the beach. She thought it was possible that Amy had hitched a ride into the city, perhaps to see me. The idea bothered her—a young woman hitching a ride on such an empty stretch of road.

162

That evening, my friend and classmate Peter K. dropped by my room on his way to the library. A stocky, pale-eyed, adventurous New Englander, Peter had just spent two years stationed in Korea in the US Army Air Defense where, in his words, he'd tried but failed to write like "T.S. Eliot among the rice paddies."

I greeted Peter and sat down on the edge of my bed. "Got a minute?" I asked, gesturing towards my desk chair. "I want to show you something."

"Something you wrote?" he asked, smiling, alert.

"No, a drawing."

"Okay," he said, sitting down.

I told Peter about Amy, my junior high school girlfriend, now a friend I often saw on vacations, about her leaving college on Sunday, sketching with her mother at Jones Beach, disappearing.

Peter had a clipped manner of speaking, almost military. "Your friend's in bad shape."

I nodded my head.

"She walked up the beach and didn't return? And nobody saw her? There's always somebody on a beach wandering around. No metal detector people?"

"All Mrs Danzer told me was they'd gotten into an argument and Amy stormed off. When she didn't return after a couple of hours, she called the state police. No trace of her. Her mother figured she'd hitched a ride into the city. Supposedly to find me. Mrs Danzer told me I was Amy's only friend—"

Peter looked up.

"I walked up and down Broadway this afternoon, looking for her, but no luck. I didn't know what else to do. A couple of weeks ago, she mailed me a drawing, which I received on Saturday. What do you make of it?"

I unfolded the drawing and laid it on my desk.

The moment has stayed with me all these years. Two young men in a small room in a gray building, a bare student's cell with its stale smells and a clanking radiator covered in paint blisters.

The cold city pressing against a black window.

Above my desk, in a cardboard frame, Sharon, like a pretty woman in an advertisement, smiled at us sweetly.

Peter looked at the drawing closely, his blond eyebrows knitted in concentration. I trusted his silences. He'd made a virtue of being alert, of noticing things. Three years older than me, he'd shipped out on freighters after college.

"This is your Volkswagen. Same hood insignia, right?" He kept his eye on the drawing.

"Yes. The drawing's a reference to a stupid joke about VWs floating. Do you see anything strange in it?"

Peter held the drawing in front of him as if he were appraising its value.

"Well," he said, "there's no driver. That's a little strange."

I nodded. There was no driver; it hadn't seemed strange before; now it did.

"Anything else?"

He stood up and placed the drawing on my desk. We both leaned over it. He pointed to the tire tracks on the dune, then tapped the drawing gently. "The car is swerving," he said. "It's out of control."

I looked closely at the driverless car. The tire tracks looked like the letter "S".

Then Peter added "Or, it might have swerved. The car might already be in the water; it's hard to tell." He pointed to the wavy lines above the dune. "Are those clouds?"

"I think so. What else could they be?"

"Waves," Peter said abruptly. "Small waves high above the car. If that's the case, then the Volkswagen isn't floating, it's sinking."

The car, I saw now, had a wavering look to it, as if it were being seen through water.

"Plummeting, actually," Peter said.

I flinched.

We were both silent for a while.

"Do you think she was trying to tell me something?"

Peter said, "Something."

Late the next morning I drove to Jones Beach with Amy's drawing beside me on the passenger seat—smudged, creased, and completely mysterious. Every time I glanced at it, new questions arose.

Around the time I passed Bellmore, I began to feel heroic, even though I was aware that self-admiration was laughably at odds with my concern for Amy. Slowly though, I began to set the stage for our imagined reunion. She'd probably have sought refuge in a dim pitch-pine thicket, behind high dunes; I'd quietly navigate around the harsh little trees, lit by splinters of sunlight, occasionally calling her name. When I'd find her, she'd be curled up against the cold, frightened and confused, but also glad to see me. The scene ended abruptly as the Jones Beach Water Tower came into view.

A few minutes later, I parked my car in the lot of Beach 6 and followed the path to the ocean. Earlier that morning, at Mrs Danzer's request, I'd stopped off to see her in Great Neck. She'd told me about Amy's last night at home, the argument with her father, her good humor the next morning, and their trip to Jones Beach to sketch. When, after sketching for an hour or so, an argument arose concerning Amy's mental health, Amy had stormed off, walking west along the shore.

I looked up and down the wide, empty beach. The winter sea was green and gray; seagulls, looking a little dirty, cruised the waves. The dunes, fenced off, were low and ordinary—beach grass, bayberry shrubs, an occasional juniper bush. No pitch-pines. No thicket. No place to hide. I walked west for half a mile, looking closely at the ocean. It was freezing that day. Could Amy have walked into *that*?

I drove back to the city, feeling deflated. How had I come up with a pitch-pine thicket?

It's odd: fifty years later I recall that Friday morning trip to Jones Beach and I remember myself walking through a thicket of little trees, looking for Amy. It's a false memory, but for unknown reasons, I can't shake it.

165

"Everything is a dream," James Salter wrote, "and only those things preserved in writing have any possibility of being real."

In the years following Amy's death, I was always on the move but I kept the sketch close at hand.

After completing my master's degree in 1965, I taught English at UNC-Greensboro for three years. In June and July I'd act in summer stock. Living lightly, I moved from one furnished apartment or trailer to another. Everything I owned was everything I wanted—a frying pan, books, record albums, a phonograph, a car, a motorcycle, and Amy's drawing. No matter where I was living I always knew which drawer it was in.

It continued to mystify me, which was perhaps Amy's intention.

Later, when I was teaching at UNC-Chapel Hill and working on a PhD., I showed the sketch to the woman I would soon marry, a funny, derisive woman from New Orleans who told me she "wasn't sentimental about the past." She said it was a very sad story, and that was that. I put it in a drawer, where it found its proper privacy.

When, some years later, I noticed that the drawing wasn't where I remembered leaving it, I began searching for it, casually at first, and then with real urgency. I turned our little box of a house inside out.

Before leaving for Greece, we'd stored our few possessions in a friend's attic. Had a box been left behind? I wanted to shout, "Amylu's drawing is missing! Which box did we put it in before we went to Crete?"

But I said nothing because by that time the "we" of our marriage was disappearing.

The drawing had been misplaced and I never found it, and I felt tainted, as if by an infidelity.

Yet once I knew it was gone, I began to dream of it, and I suppose that's what I recall most vividly—a document that floats occasionally in and out of dreams.

I called my friend Peter K. yesterday and asked him if he remembered Amy's drawing. "No," he said, "not the specifics, but I remember we looked at it. And you've talked to me about it over the years. So I guess I remember it."

Recently I dusted off the large books on the top shelf of my bedroom bookcase. Carrying them outside, I blew little clouds of dust into the ivy. Naturally, once I held the books in my hand, the old calculations kicked in. When had I bought Norman Mailer's *Marilyn*? Before my first wife and I went to Crete? After we'd returned? And what about Meyer Schapiro's lavish *Cézanne* with its elegant cover of burnished apples and oranges? Surely, even in a hurry, I wouldn't have stuck a soiled charcoal drawing between its gorgeous plates.

And even if I'd found it, even if I'd held it in my hands—the only work of art that was created for me alone—would anything have become clearer?

Nothing has ever been clear.

Charcoal in hand, sketchpad on her lap, she drew a drowning car.

I thought it was a joke. Then I thought it wasn't.

Was it an entreaty?

Was it her way of saying, Enough?

Maybe it was a joke. Lolita wasn't underwater. Those were clouds, not waves. Peter was wrong. She was just rushing down the dune to float with us, the only airtight car in the world.

How many questions am I allowed to ask in a lifetime?

No one needs to tell me how pointless, even vaporous, these old questions and speculations are. I'm like a retired cop who wakes up in the night and runs through the minute details of an old crime that nobody else remembers. I don't do it very often, because, as I said, it's pointless. But I do it now and then. I say to myself: Amy mailed it on February 10th and I received it ten days later. If she'd included a return address on her envelope, it would have been returned to her for insufficient postage. She would have known that I'd never received it. But she didn't know that.

She thought I'd received and hadn't responded.

Why would someone not respond to a drawing someone had sent them? A drawing is a significant form of communication. There's only one answer: indifference

It wouldn't have crossed Amylu's mind that there might have been a postage problem.

I'm not a fool. I know these old questions have no meaning in the real world. Still, they're mine.

So I ask myself, where did I put it? How could I have lost it? *How could I have lost it?*

I dreamed that I was having an argument with a strange and beautiful and complicated woman who may or may not have been in love with me. We were staying in a house by the sea, this woman and I, and we were arguing about the feasibility of buying this house. She left the room for a moment and I looked out the window towards the ocean, a window that was like a vertical black-and-white photograph, and for a moment it was a black-and-white photograph—for a white dazzling moon was shining behind dark passionate clouds onto a bone-white beach—only the image was alive and full of wild beauty. When I called to the woman to come quick, she did, but by that time everything was back to normal, and we were simply tourists again looking at beachfront property, wondering if we should buy it.

from *"Dreaming of Paradise"*

NPR Commentary by John Rosenthal on WUNC-FM, 1986

CAMUS

I always kind of blamed Camus and the other existentialists for Amylu's death because a few days before she left school she asked me about the opening line of Camus' The Myth of Sisyphus—*"The only important philosophical decision is whether to commit suicide or not."*

From a 1992 letter from Lucy W,
a classmate of Amy's at RISD 1962–1965

Yes, it's possible that Amy was touched, like many other young people in the early 1960s, by the existentialists: Camus, for instance, who insisted on life without consolation. But suicide itself is not meaningless or a sign of derangement. Can one possibly imagine the emotions—the courage, the pain, the determination, the despair—of a free soul making that rendezvous with death?

Email, October, 2016, from Mike Fink,
English Professor, RISD

Albert Camus and Amylu. I'd like to believe it's not true, that it overstates the influence of a few words. After all, there were plenty of college students in 1965 who were inspired by Camus to declare that life was meaningless, though very few really believed it. Then again, very few of them sat on the floor in a winter coat for hours and hours—as Beatrice M. described Amy—saying nothing. And very few had ever descended into what Lucy described as Amy's "inner battle zone." What if Amylu had discovered that she didn't have the courage or the talent to go deep enough within to find whatever her professors insisted must be found if one is to make art that matters? Who was around to tell her that her teachers might be wrong, or that making art isn't the only thing that matters?

DAUGHTER OF THE AIR

In the early spring of 1985, I was working in my darkroom on a photograph I'd taken a few weeks earlier in Central Park. On that February day, a gray day, I'd wandered down Central Park West and turned into the park at 65th Street. As the afternoon light faded I walked through a deserted children's playground not far from Columbus Circle. Suddenly it began to snow—a thick snow that fell like feathers. In a matter of moments everything in the park had turned lacy and mysterious. Shielding my camera under my coat, I checked the exposure, knowing the snow would hold the light for a few extra minutes. Then I slipped into the zone of silence where photographs are found. Breathing deeply, I saw three bare patches of black cement under the seats of three snow-dusted swings. A winter lyric, with half-notes.

Now, weeks later in the darkroom, Dylan's "Idiot Wind" playing in the background, I looked at the photograph under the enlarger. The bare, whitening park, the three snowless patches. And something wrong: the seat of the middle swing was askew, tilting—a useless swing.

As the afternoon wore on, and I fell into the rhythm of familiar work, I remembered the rope swing that had hung from a large branch in Amy's backyard. A relic of childhood.

Amylu, I thought, would now be in her early forties—a pale, blond woman with blue eyes that narrowed when she laughed. I couldn't quite picture her—not an aged Amylu. My memories of her, of which there were fewer each year, were like a small exhibi-

173

tion of still photographs. Her face next to mine at Jones Beach, her cheek caked with sand; her flushed face beneath a silly beanie on MacDougal Street, her breath condensing in the cold air. In dreams I could re-capture a lively Amylu, but it was a slightly skewed Amylu upon whose laughter and admiration I could no longer count. Sometimes, though, in the darkroom, when the ordinary world was silent and reveries floated above the sound of running water, she seemed close by and familiar. For instance, what would she think of this photograph?

Well, the answer was obvious to me: she would take it in all at once, silently, approvingly—the snow, the solitude, the distilled air, the tilted seat; she'd know in her bones that a child sitting on a tilted seat will always slide into the pinch; she'd feel the pinch. And she would hear the absent children's voices, which was the secret of the photograph, beyond the silence of the falling snow.

More than a quarter of a century has passed since I worked in my darkroom on that Central Park photograph, communing with Amy as if her suicide were a brief interruption of our friendship, a wrinkle that could be brushed away. That's not so strange or unusual, is it? The unexpected suicide of a close friend is humiliating; it ruins the present and muddles the past; it refutes everything—the here-and-now, common memories, candor, shared music, remembered laughter. It's so large a fact that it can't be taken in all at once. Not by half. So one resorts to magical thinking, to an alternative reality. My friend killed herself ... but not really.

Is this kind of wistfulness too irrational to be taken seriously? I don't think so. Rationality rarely takes into account the tremulous imaginings that underlie our emotional life, and which, even more than our actions, shape our unique personalities. Rationality doesn't measure the indwelling force of the dead who helped or hindered us. Nor does our memory of them, which remains active and vivid and welcoming even though they are gone, come to standstill because they rejected us in the last fraction of their life. Memory doesn't work that way.

If Amy had managed to survive, I said to myself as I worked in the darkroom in 1985, we would have been the best of friends. Decades later I ask different questions. Did I ever know her? Did I even try to know her? Was I capable then of really knowing another person, or was I too distracted by the restless shimmering of my own self-regard? "It's not so far that you can't see me!" she'd said angrily on the day of our last visit. But, as it turned out, it was too far. I didn't see her, even as she walked, half-dazed, beside me.

Do I see her now?

Yes, I get it, it's too late.

Nonetheless, I'm still standing here as the threat of oblivion settles over her memory. I'm still wondering what she was thinking as she moved toward the waves. I'm still asking myself, was she emptied of meaning, or too full of it? Was she mentally ill, or in Thomas Szasz's deeply humane phrase, "disabled by living?"

Was she angry, lost, hurt, confused, depressed, mentally ill? Did she take the wrong class? Read the wrong books? Fear the hollowness of words? Curse a world where complacencies rule and nothing is safe from contradiction?

Was she longing for the unattainable? According to one of her classmates at RISD, she built a sand castle and walked into the sea.

Does any of this matter anymore?

She was twenty. Her suicide has been going on for half a century, yet she remains twenty. I want to say to her "Amy, why didn't you ..." But she was twenty.

This I know: Amylu was not the same thing as her suicide.

So there she was in 1985, a familiar spirit, leaning over my shoulder in the dark, twenty years after her death, nodding her head in approval while Dylan sang "Idiot Wind" in the background. No, Amylu whispered in the amber darkness, the photograph isn't esoteric, private, obtuse, it's just the opposite. A swing is part of the architecture of childhood. It's universal. Do you remember the swing in my back yard?

Was Amylu standing beside me because I was unwilling to face the dreadful fact of suicide, or because death itself, in the memory of the living, is just another form of leave-taking? I don't know. Whatever the answer, it's a terrible paradox that because Amy died at twenty—before we had time, perhaps, in the usual way of things, to embark upon the long-term project of forgetting each other—her sweet gaze still endures.

Acknowledgments

My thanks to the several people without whose interest and encouragement over the years this book would still be a work in progress: Chris Frost, Peter Keville, Alan Shapiro, David Summer, Mike Fink, Alan Dehmer, Daniel Wallace, Greg Conniff, John Keats Rosenthal, Allen Ruppersberg, Joy Javits, Andy Fleishman, Laura Press, Myles Ludwig, the late Dr Wallace Jackson, the late Bill Walton, and my wife, Paula Press, who was there from beginning to end.

And special thanks to the people whose editorial guidance helped me realize the book I wanted to write: Jay Tolson, Masie Cochran, Pam Durban, Ann Loftin, Peggy Payne, my Waywiser editor, Philip Hoy, and Sheron Dailey, my first reader.

And a final thanks to Nick Garland for a very welcome late suggestion.

A Note About the Author

John Rosenthal was born in New York City in 1942. He received his B.A. from Wake Forest College in 1964, and an M.A. in English Literature from Columbia University in 1966. He taught English at the University of North Carolina–Chapel Hill until 1971 when he left teaching to become an essayist and a photographer. His work has been widely exhibited in the United States, including exhibitions at The National Humanities Center, The National Academy of Sciences in Washington D.C., and Boston's Panopticon Gallery. His articles have appeared in many journals and magazines, amongst them *The Sun Magazine, Five Points* and *The Huffington Post*. In 1998 a collection of Mr. Rosenthal's photographs, *Regarding Manhattan,* was published by Safe Harbor Books, and in 2015 Safe Harbor published his 2007 collection of New Orleans photographs, *AFTER: The Silence of the Lower 9th Ward*. In the 1990s, Mr. Rosenthal was a regular commentator on NPR's *All Things Considered*.

Other Books from Waywiser

POETRY

Austin Allen, *Pleasures of the Game*
Al Alvarez, *New & Selected Poems*
Chris Andrews, *Lime Green Chair*
Audrey Bohanan, *Any Keep or Contour*
George Bradley, *A Few of Her Secrets*
Geoffrey Brock, *Voices Bright Flags*
Christopher Cessac, *The Youngest Ocean*
Robert Conquest, *Blokelore & Blokesongs*
Robert Conquest, *Collected Poems*
Robert Conquest, *Penultimata*
Morri Creech, *Blue Rooms*
Morri Creech, *Field Knowledge*
Morri Creech, *The Sleep of Reason*
Peter Dale, *One Another*
James Davis, *Club Q*
Erica Dawson, *Big-Eyed Afraid*
B. H. Fairchild, *The Art of the Lathe*
David Ferry, *On This Side of the River: Selected Poems*
Daniel Groves & Greg Williamson, eds., *Jiggery-Pokery Semicentennial*
Jeffrey Harrison, *The Names of Things: New & Selected Poems*
Joseph Harrison, *Identity Theft*
Joseph Harrison, *Shakespeare's Horse*
Joseph Harrison, *Someone Else's Name*
Joseph Harrison, *Sometimes I Dream That I Am Not Walt Whitman*
Joseph Harrison, ed., *The Hecht Prize Anthology, 2005-2009*
Anthony Hecht, *Collected Later Poems*
Anthony Hecht, *The Darkness and the Light*
Jaimee Hills, *How to Avoid Speaking*
Katherine Hollander, *My German Dictionary*
Hilary S. Jacqmin, *Missing Persons*
Carrie Jerrell, *After the Revival*
Stephen Kampa, *Articulate as Rain*
Stephen Kampa, *Bachelor Pad*
Rose Kelleher, *Bundle o' Tinder*
Mark Kraushaar, *The Uncertainty Principle*
Matthew Ladd, *The Book of Emblems*
William Logan, *Old Flame: New Selected Poems, 1974–2012*
J. D. McClatchy, *Plundered Hearts: New and Selected Poems*
Dora Malech, *Shore Ordered Ocean*
Jérôme Luc Martin, *The Gardening Fires: Sonnets and Fragments*
Eric McHenry, *Odd Evening*
Eric McHenry, *Potscrubber Lullabies*
Eric McHenry and Nicholas Garland, *Mommy Daddy Evan Sage*
Timothy Murphy, *Very Far North*
Ian Parks, *Shell Island*
V. Penelope Pelizzon, *Whose Flesh is Flame, Whose Bone is Time*
Chris Preddle, *Cattle Console Him*
Shelley Puhak, *Guinevere in Baltimore*

Christopher Ricks, ed., *Joining Music with Reason:
34 Poets, British and American, Oxford 2004-2009*
Daniel Rifenburgh, *Advent*

Other Books from Waywiser

Mary Jo Salter, *It's Hard to Say: Selected Poems*
W. D. Snodgrass, *Not for Specialists: New & Selected Poems*
Mark Strand, *Almost Invisible*
Mark Strand, *Blizzard of One*
Bradford Gray Telford, *Perfect Hurt*
Matthew Thorburn, *This Time Tomorrow*
Cody Walker, *Shuffle and Breakdown*
Cody Walker, *The Self-Styled No-Child*
Cody Walker, *The Trumpiad*
Deborah Warren, *The Size of Happiness*
Clive Watkins, *Already the Flames*
Clive Watkins, *Jigsaw*
Richard Wilbur, *Anterooms*
Richard Wilbur, *Mayflies*
Richard Wilbur, *Collected Poems 1943-2004*
Norman Williams, *One Unblinking Eye*
Greg Williamson, *A Most Marvelous Piece of Luck*
Greg Williamson, *The Hole Story of Kirby the Sneak and Arlo the True*
Stephen Yenser, *Stone Fruit*

FICTION
Gregory Heath, *The Entire Animal*
Mary Elizabeth Pope, *Divining Venus*
K. M. Ross, *The Blinding Walk*
Gabriel Roth, *The Unknowns**
Matthew Yorke, *Chancing It*

ILLUSTRATED
Nicholas Garland, *I wish ...*
Eric McHenry and Nicholas Garland, *Mommy Daddy Evan Sage*
Greg Williamson, *The Hole Story of Kirby the Sneak and Arlo the True*

NON-FICTION
Neil Berry, *Articles of Faith: The Story of British Intellectual Journalism*
Irving Feldman, *Usable Truths: Aphorisms & Observations*
Mark Ford, *A Driftwood Altar: Essays and Reviews*
Philip Hoy, ed., *A Bountiful Harvest:*
The Correspondence of Anthony Hecht and William L. MacDonald
Richard Wollheim, *Germs: A Memoir of Childhood*

* Co-published with Picador